Leadership U.
Preparing Students for College, Career, and Beyond

Leadership U.
Preparing Students for College, Career, and Beyond

High School Supplement

Your Passport to College: Practical Support for the College Application Process

Copyright © 2020 The Leadership Program

All rights reserved.

No part of this book may be reproduced, or stored in a retrieval system, or transmitted in any form or by any means, electronic, mechanical, photocopying, recording, or otherwise, without express written permission of the publisher.

Created by The Leadership Program, New York
www.theleadershipprogram.com

The Leadership Program
535 8th Avenue, Floor 16
New York, NY 10018

 **GIRL FRIDAY BOOKS**

Published by Girl Friday Books™, Seattle
www.girlfridaybooks.com

Produced by Girl Friday Productions

ISBN (paperback): 978-1-959411-10-9

Printed in the United States of America

Contents

Introduction: Overview vii

Workshop One: Destination and Equipment 1
Objective: *Students will learn the benefits of obtaining a college degree, the difference between types of institutions of higher learning, how to identify their post–high school graduation plans, and what is needed to apply to college.*

Workshop Two: Itinerary and Timeline 19
Objective: *Students will gain an understanding of the college admission process as well as the steps for completing college applications.*

Workshop Three: College Essays, Part 1 41
Objective: *Students examine the Common App essay prompts, select their prompts, and learn what colleges are looking for in a well-written, responsive essay.*

Workshop Four: College Essays, Part 2 57
Objective: *Students will learn essay strategies, structures, and best practices for writing a Common App essay.*

Workshop Five: FAFSA, Part 1 69
Objective: *Students will learn the what, why, when, and how of completing the FAFSA and the basics of financial aid.*

Workshop Six: FAFSA, Part 2 83
Objective: *Students will learn the difference between institutional and external scholarships and the role the FAFSA plays in applying for funds. Students will also learn how to strategically search for additional funding.*

Workshop Seven: Parents 91
Objective: *Parents and families will learn the roles they can play to best assist their students during the college application process and the importance of the FAFSA. They will begin to visualize their children as college students.*

Theoretical Rationale 105
References 107
Image Credits 108
Program Curriculum Support 109

Introduction

Overview

THE LEADERSHIP PROGRAM: WHO WE ARE

For over twenty years, The Leadership Program has worked to provide educational institutions of all types and sizes with youth development activities, professional development workshops, and curricula that help schools expand and enrich their academic communities.

Based in New York City, we serve more than 250 school administrations and organizations nationwide and internationally; we have worked tirelessly to create innovative and engaging curricula that provide schools assistance with youth engagement, parent involvement, management, organization, educational enrichment, strategic planning, and evaluation of their team.

We are highly regarded in the realm of educational consulting and professional development, and are regularly invited to present at national conferences on topics ranging from social-emotional learning to motivating your staff.

The Leadership Program:
- works with over 18,000 students, 500 teachers, and 6,000 parents annually
- created and implements a conflict-resolution project that has been designated the highest-rated leadership-themed universal adolescent violence prevention program in the country by SAMHSA's National Registry of Evidence-Based Programs and Practices (NREPP)
- created an empirically validated Conflict Resolution Project, one of thirty-five in the country and designated a Promising Program by the Office of Juvenile Justice and Delinquency Prevention
- was included in a 2008 Johns Hopkins research study for the Department of Defense as one of five organizations in the United States that significantly enhances positive school culture through professional development, organization, and youth development
- created two of the seven programs in New York State (two of the seventy-three in the nation) designated to have Promising Practices by the Academy for Educational Development
- has its conflict resolution curriculum listed as a CASEL "SELect" effective SEL skills development program
- believes that, with the right help, every person has the innate ability to lead the change

CURRICULUM OVERVIEW

Welcome to Leadership U., The Leadership Program's comprehensive, multi-year college and career readiness series that prepares students from elementary grades through high school for higher education and beyond. This differentiated curriculum is structured to develop age-appropriate skills in youth that will support them in attending college, thriving in higher education or alternative advanced training, and planning for successful careers as adults. To that end, the manuals are organized as follows:

- 4th–5th grades
- 6th–8th grades
- 9th–10th grades
- 11th–12th grades
- 11th–12th grade Your Passport to College Supplement

The curriculum lessons, focusing on SEL and practical life skills, are organized into a series of components that engage students in a variety of activities and are scaffolded to develop their awareness of and belief in college as an option for themselves, their curiosity about and embrace of diverse cultures, their ability to work with others constructively, their SEL competencies for managing emotions and recovering from setbacks, and real-world skills such as money and time management. All lessons include vital time to reflect on what they have learned.

This teacher manual, and the corresponding manuals for each grade level, support both experienced and beginning facilitators in implementing Leadership U. lessons.

Your Passport to College
Leadership's Your Passport to College curriculum supports students through the nuts and bolts of the college application process. Building on our proven-effective approach to enrichment and SEL development, this supplement uses interactive activities to examine the why, where, and how of applying to college, identify pertinent requirements and deadlines, further develop problem-solving skills, and help students to envision a realistic college experience tailored to their needs, skill level, and interests. With these factors in mind, students will be guided through the process of completing college applications and FAFSA financial aid forms, and writing their application essays with confidence and clarity.

Main Components for Your Passport to College

- Destination and Equipment
- Itinerary and Timeline
- College Essays, Part 1
- College Essays, Part 2
- FAFSA, Part 1
- FAFSA, Part 2
- Parents

Workshop One

Destination and Equipment

YOUR PASSPORT TO COLLEGE

Destination and Equipment

OBJECTIVE:
Students will learn the benefits of obtaining a college degree, the difference between types of institutions of higher learning, how to identify their post–high school graduation plans, and what is needed to apply to college. Then they will begin to visualize themselves as college students.

SUMMARY:
Through a passport analogy, students will learn the benefits of attending college and obtaining a college degree, identify different types of institutions, develop their postgraduation plans, and visualize themselves as college co-eds.

MATERIALS:
*AV equipment for PowerPoint presentation (download the file from www.tlpnyc.com/your-passport-to-college), stable internet connection, and one student handout (**Destination and Equipment**)*

Lesson Vocabulary

associate's degree n. a degree awarded upon completion of a two-year course of study at a two-year institution

bachelor's degree n. a college degree usually completed in four years of full-time study; most common are bachelor of arts (BA), awarded to students who major in the arts and humanities, and bachelor of science (BS), awarded to students who major in science, technology, or business

four-year institution n. public or private colleges and universities with undergraduate degree programs that lead to a bachelor's degree in a specific area of study

gap year n. typically a year-long break immediately after high school and before college during which students engage in various educational and developmental activities, such as travel or some type of regular work

HBCU (Historically Black Colleges and Universities) n. a college or university whose principal mission is to educate black students, although it is open to all students; there are currently 107 in existence

two-year institution n. a public or private college that provides two-year courses of study that end with students earning an associate's degree; sometimes referred to as a junior or community college and may include a vocational school or technical college

vocational school n. an educational institution whose mission is to equip students with skills needed to enter the workforce by training them for a specific line of work; less academic and more job-focused than a four-year institution

FACILITATOR NOTE:
Familiarize yourself with the fourteen slides in this lesson, including the embedded videos, prior to facilitation. Make copies of handouts for students.

WARM-UP: PASSPORT ANALOGY

- Ask students whether they have been or know anyone who has been out of the country.
- Follow-up by asking whether they know what document or item is required to leave the United States to visit another country. (Correct answer: passport.)
- Proceed to explain what a passport is and how one is used. Keep the explanation short: a passport is a travel document issued by the US government that identifies you and authorizes you to travel internationally; upon arrival in a new country, you will have your passport stamped by an immigration official with the country's seal.
- Tell students that passports provide access to the world and exposure to new places and different people the same way that college provides access to a whole new world and exposure to different places and people. This is true even for those students who choose to attend college locally.
- Tell students that completing these workshops will be like their "passport" to college and that they should keep their notes all in one place.

MAIN ACTIVITY

Part 1: Destination

- Begin PowerPoint presentation. Stay on **slide #1**.
- Ask students to identify some of the benefits of having a college degree.
- Present and review content in **slide #2: Why Go to College?**
- Highlight the following while on this slide:
  - <u>Increased access to job opportunities</u>: College graduates see 57 percent more job opportunities than nongraduates, and it's estimated that two-thirds of all jobs currently require postsecondary education.
  - <u>Increased earning potential</u>: Education beyond high school leads to increased salaries. Lifetime earnings are as follows: $520,000—no high school diploma; $712,000 with high school diploma; $836,000 with an associate's degree; and $1,173,000 with a bachelor's degree.
- Inform students that they are preparing to learn about applying to college and that it will be similar to going on a trip.
- Ask students what is the first thing that they need to go on a trip. (Correct answer: a destination.)

- Tell students that in addition to a destination, or somewhere to go, there are three other things they will need to take a trip.
- Present **slide #3**. Using the wording on the slide, describe each of the four things students will need: Destination, Equipment, Timeline, and Route or Itinerary.
- Remind students that their destination is college.
- Tell students that just as a passport allows travelers to go to different countries, students get to choose different colleges.
- Present **slide #4**.
- Tell students that you will talk about their available postgraduation destinations, but the focus will be on four-year colleges.
- Define a four-year institution for students.
- Tell students that when they hear people speak of college, this is more than likely the type of college they are referring to.
- Seek student participation by asking students to provide the names of four-year colleges that they've heard of.
- Introduce the acronym HBCU (Historically Black Colleges and Universities) and tell students that these are four-year institutions whose primary mission is to educate black students, although any student is permitted to attend. Provide the following examples: Howard University (Washington, DC); Hampton University (Hampton, VA); North Carolina A&T State University (Greensboro, NC); Spelman College (all female—Atlanta, GA); and Morehouse College (all male—Atlanta, GA).
- Define a two-year institution and tell students that they are sometimes called community or junior colleges and that some are technical colleges.
- Present **slide #5** and tell participants they are going to watch a brief video (3:33) on the differences between the types of colleges (two-year vs. four-year vs. technical).
- Encourage students to pursue a college education even if they are the first in their families to do so. Stress that college is within reach.
- Tell students there are 3,330+ four-year public and private colleges (excluding for-profit institutions) in the United States. There is a place for everyone.
- Present **slide #6: Student Success** and watch the video (12:15) of students sharing their experiences of going to college.
- Ask participants to name alternatives to college that a student can pursue after high school graduation.
- Tell students that three alternative postgraduation options exist.
- Present **slide #7: Alternative Destinations** and discuss each option. Keep discussion of a gap year short by providing the definition and only a few examples, such as hiking the Appalachian Trail in its entirety, volunteering at an animal sanctuary, or studying a martial art and taking language classes in a foreign country. Feel free to provide your own example(s).

- Mention that students interested in joining the military can go to college on an ROTC scholarship. ROTC is a college program offered at over 1,700 colleges and universities that prepares students to become officers in the US military. In exchange for a paid college education and a postgraduation career, students agree to serve in the military after graduation.
- Encourage students to discuss their postgraduation plans with their guidance counselors or other trusted adults who know them well.
- Present **slide #8: Takeaways!**
  - Remember that each student is different.
  - Create the best plan for YOU.
  - First-generation students can and do succeed in college.

Part 2: Equipment

- Present **slide #9: Equipment**. Now that students have a destination (college), tell them that just as they need a suitcase for a trip, they will need "equipment" to apply to college.
- Inform students that they will need five pieces of equipment: a transcript, test scores, records, a resume or activity list, and "other stuff."
  - Transcript: Advise students that a transcript is a record of their high school grades. Sometimes it is known as a report card. Tell them that they will request their guidance counselors send their transcripts directly to the colleges they apply to. It will not cost anything.
    - Encourage students to take challenging classes because colleges like students to challenge themselves. Colleges call it "rigor."
  - Test scores: Tell students that although not all colleges require test scores, the vast majority do. Colleges that do not require test scores are called "test optional." Advise students that there is a website that maintains a list of test-optional colleges. It is www.fairtest.org, and it is included in the resources section for this workshop.
    - Tell students that they will need to take either the SAT or ACT and receive their scores, ideally, no later than the early fall of their senior year. This does not mean waiting until senior year to take either test. Students should ideally take either test during their junior year. Plan for re-testing, if necessary.
- Present **slide #10**. Review the comparison overview of the ACT and SAT.
  - ACT subjects: English, Math, Reading, and Science
  - SAT sections: Evidence-Based Reading, Writing, and Math
- Inform students that the ACT and SAT are substantively very different tests. Let them know that there is a helpful video (approx. 12 min.) that they can view to learn about the differences. The video is included in the resources for this lesson. Encourage students to seek advice from a teacher, counselor, or other trusted adult if they need help deciding which test to take.

- Tell students where they can register and the costs for the tests as provided on the slide.
- Instruct students to speak with their counselors ASAP if they need to request a fee waiver.
- Tell students that if they are eligible for an ACT fee waiver, they have access to a plethora of free learning services. Resources with details regarding both the ACT and SAT fee waivers are included in this lesson.
- Present **slide #11**. Advise students that there are FREE online test prep resources available.
- Stress to students that the importance of practice cannot be overstated. Standardized test-taking is a skill, and all skills require practice.
- Encourage students to ask their guidance counselors for additional resources. In addition, tell students to speak with their counselors if they need special accommodations for testing, such as extended time. (Note: This may be of particular interest to students with IEPs and/or 504 plans.)
- Restate the first two pieces of "equipment" students will need, transcripts and test scores.
- Present **slide #12**. Tell students that they will also need to gather certain information. This information makes up their <u>records</u>.
- Tell students that they should make a list of any of the following they have done in 9th–12th grades: community service, including dates and locations; awards; places of employment, including dates; significant projects; and extracurricular involvement.
- Tell students that it is not necessary to have a <u>resume</u>, but that having one would be helpful. Some college admission and scholarship applications accept them.
- Review. Ask students to name the first four pieces of equipment they need. (Correct answer: transcript, test scores, records, and resume.)
- Present **slide #13**. Tell students that the "<u>other</u>" equipment they may need are letters of recommendation, essays, and portfolios. Not all colleges require one or all of these items.
- Explain to students that they will be responsible for asking teachers, counselors, coaches, or other adults who know them well to write letters on their behalf.
- Tell students that if a college requires an essay as part of the application process, an essay prompt will be provided. If an essay is optional, it is best to submit one.
- Tell students that the vast majority of students will not have to create portfolios. They are typically only required for students applying to specific majors, such as architecture, art, or photography.
- Present **slide #14: Takeaways!**

DISCUSSION QUESTIONS

1. *How do I envision myself immediately after graduation?*
2. *Have I spoken with my school counselor about my postgraduation plans?*

CLOSING

- After graduation, I see myself _____.
- People that I can go to for help with applying to college include _____.

EXTENSION ACTIVITY

- Tell students to start working on their lists of activities, awards, employment, community service, and extracurricular activities. Instruct them to update this list as new information becomes available and to hang on to it until it is time to begin their college applications. A hard copy or an electronic list is acceptable. This list can also be used to create a resume.

RESOURCES

- https://youtu.be/yXPwtO72CR0: Video (11:49) that explains the differences between the SAT and ACT and provides considerations students should think about when deciding which test to take
- https://youtu.be/8TwZ8o8jnQU: Video (1:20) of Michelle Obama encouraging students to work hard to create more opportunities to go to college and asking them to commit to continuing their education past high school
- www.mass.edu/gearup/documents/WritingaResume.pdf: Sample high school resume with instructions
- https://blog.collegeboard.org/guide-to-sat-fee-waivers: Detailed information on SAT fee waivers
- www.act.org/content/dam/act/unsecured/documents/R1826-fee-waiver-usage.pdf: Detailed information on ACT fee waivers
- www.fairtest.org: Maintains a list of test-optional colleges and universities
- Instagram and Twitter:
    - @actstudent—ACT
    - @collegeboard—SAT
- www.mynextmove.org: Tool from the US Department of Labor designed to help young adults, students, and workers explore careers and find jobs
- https://imfirst.org: Provides inspiration, information, and support on the road to and through college for first-generation students

NAME: _____

WORKSHOP ONE: DESTINATION AND EQUIPMENT

Take time to complete each of the exercises, answer all of the questions, and write plenty of notes.

My destination: _____

Four things I will need to get to college:
(1) D_____
(2) E_____
(3) R_____
(4) T_____

Types of "equipment" I will need to apply to college:
(1) T_____
(2) T_____
(3) R_____
(4) R_____
(5) O_____

FREE Test Prep Resources
ACT—www._____
SAT—www._____

Test-taking is a skill, and all skills require _____.

QUESTIONS

1. *How do I envision myself immediately after graduation?*
2. *Have I spoken with my school counselor about my postgraduation plans?*

PLANNING AHEAD

- After graduation, I see myself _____
  _____.
- People that I can go to for help with applying to college include _____
  _____.

EXERCISES

- In 9th through 12th grades, I have participated in, received, or done the following:
    - ○ Activities
    - ○ Awards
    - ○ Employment
    - ○ Community service
    - ○ Extracurricular activities

NOTES

_____
_____
_____
_____
_____
_____
_____
_____
_____
_____
_____
_____
_____
_____
_____
_____
_____
_____
_____

ANSWERS

WORKSHOP ONE: DESTINATION AND EQUIPMENT

Four things I will need to get to college:

(1) D_____ Destination

(2) E_____ Equipment

(3) R_____ Route or Itinerary

(4) T_____ Timeline

Types of "equipment" I will need to apply to college:

(1) T_____ Transcript

(2) T_____ Test scores

(3) R_____ Records

(4) R_____ Resume

(5) O_____ Other

FREE Test Prep Resources

ACT—www.___academy.act.org___

SAT—www.___khanacademy.org___

Test-taking is a skill, and all skills require _____practice_____.

Slide #1

Slide #2

Why Go to College?

1. Increased access to job opportunities
2. Preparation for a specialized career
3. Increased marketability
4. Increased earning potential
5. Economic stability
6. Networking opportunities
7. A pathway to advancement
8. Personal growth and improved self-esteem
9. Higher job satisfaction
10. Positive return on investment

Source: Northeastern University

Slide #3

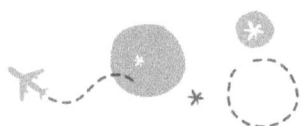

Destination—Where do you want to go?

Equipment—What will you need to get there?

Route or Itinerary—How do you want to get there?

Timeline—When do you want to get there?

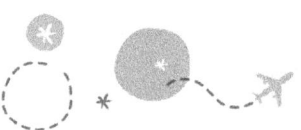

Slide #4

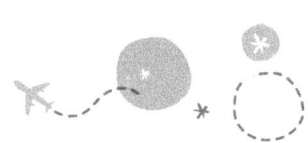 **Destination:** College

What's the Difference?

Four-year institution
Two-year institution

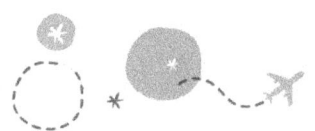

Slide #5

Colleges: Vocational, Two-year, and Four-year

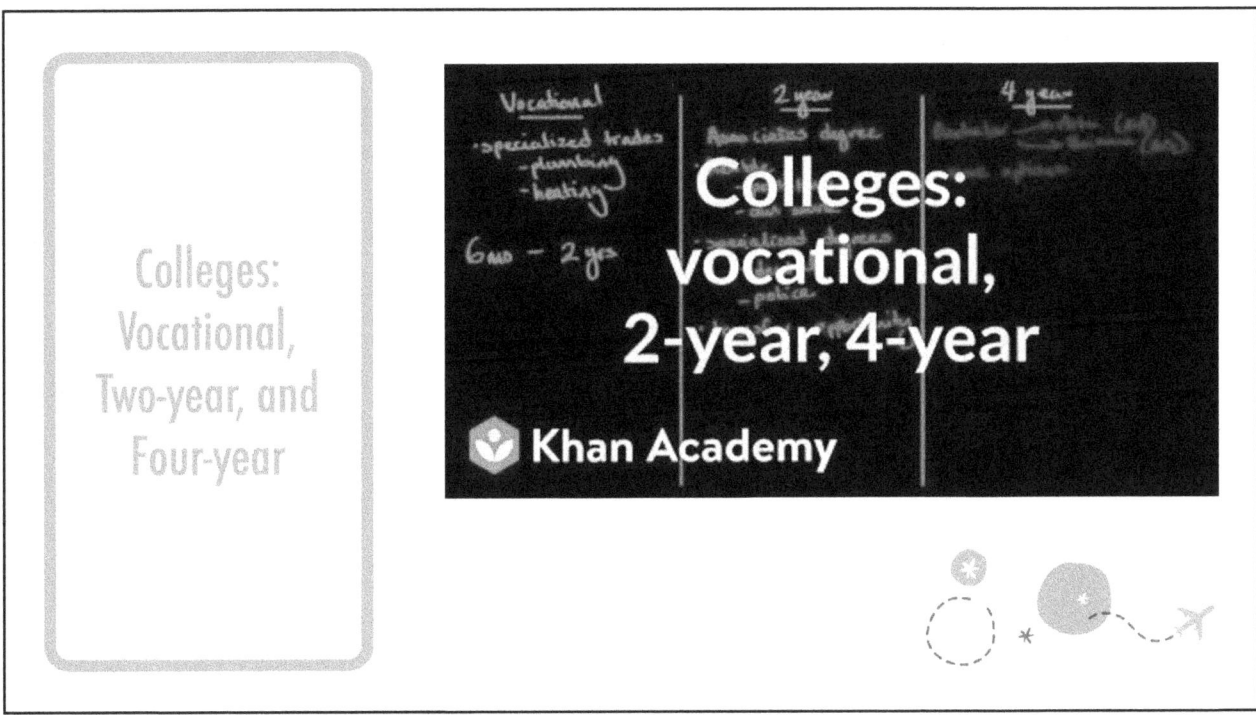

Slide #6

Student Success

Slide #7

Slide #8

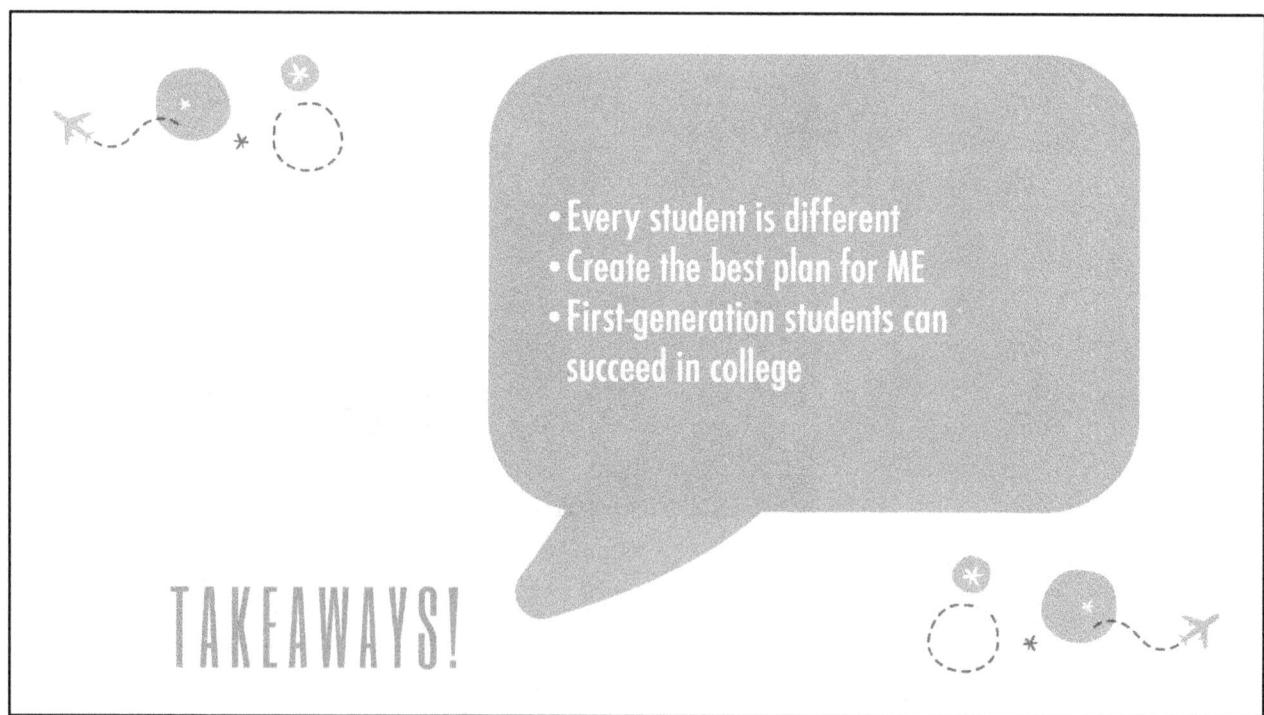

Slide #9

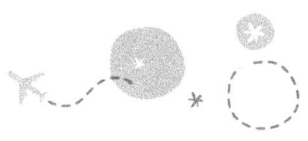

Equipment

- Transcript
- Test scores
- Records
- Resume
- Other

Slide #10

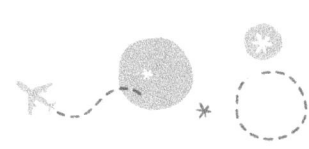

Equipment: Test Scores

ACT	SAT
4 subjects + optional essay	3 subjects + optional essay
2 hrs 55 min + 40 min for optional essay	3 hrs 50 min + 50 min for optional essay
215 questions	154 questions
offered 7 times per year	offered 7 times per year
perfect score: 36	perfect score: 1600
no penalty for wrong answers	no penalty for wrong answers
Registration: www.act.org	Registration: www.collegeboard.org
Cost: $55 without essay; $70 with essay	Cost: $52 without essay; $68 with essay
IG and Twitter: @actstudent	IG and Twitter: @collegeboard

Slide #11

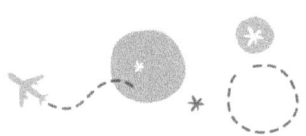

FREE Test Prep Resources

ACT — ACT Academy — www.academy.act.org

SAT — www.khanacademy.org

Test-taking is a skill, and all skills require practice

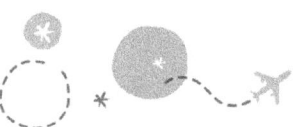

Slide #12

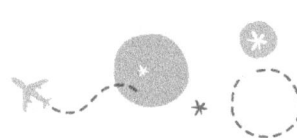

Equipment: Records

- Community service
- Awards
- Employment
- Significant projects
- Extracurricular activities

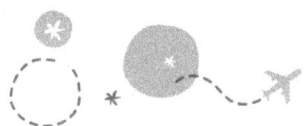

Slide #13

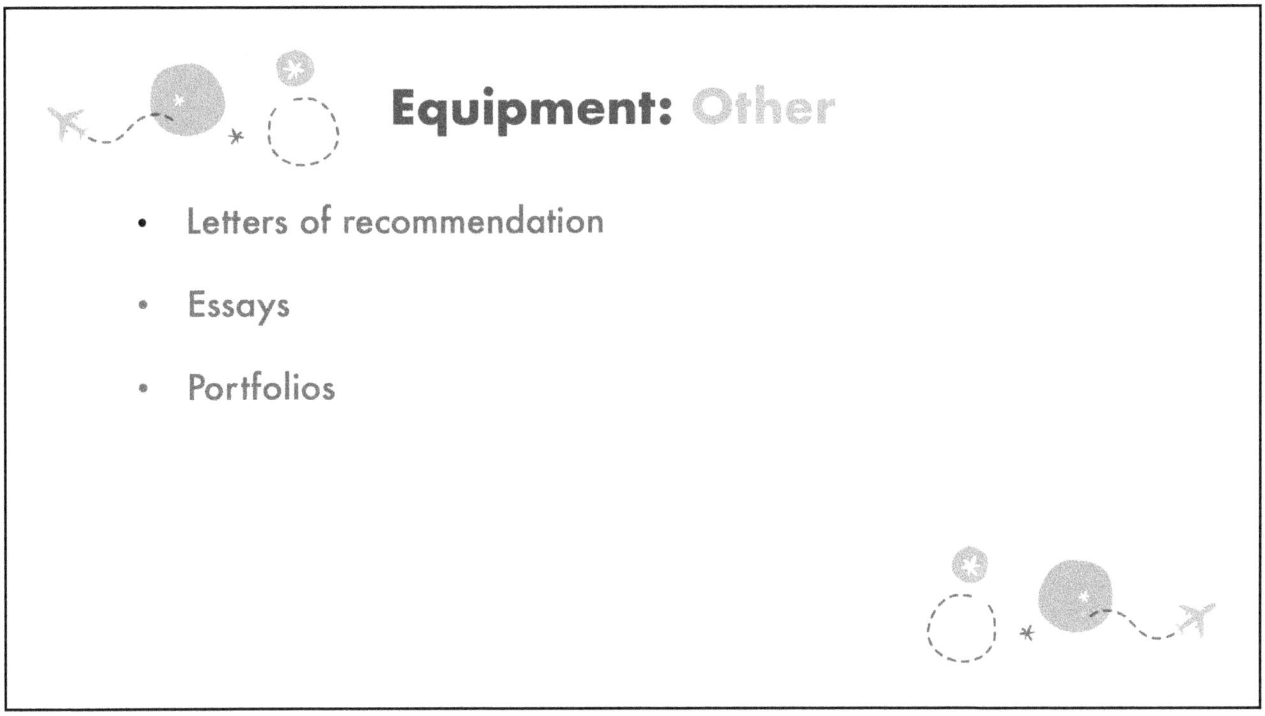

Equipment: Other

- Letters of recommendation
- Essays
- Portfolios

Slide #14

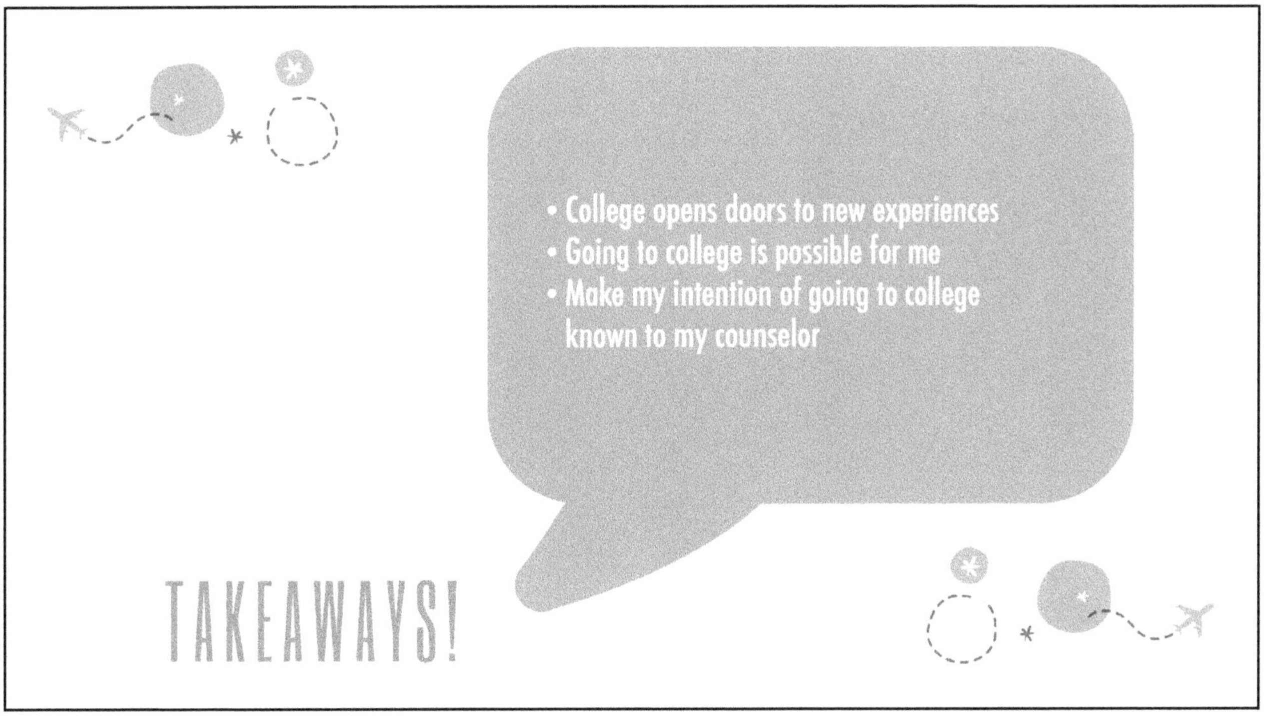

TAKEAWAYS!

- College opens doors to new experiences
- Going to college is possible for me
- Make my intention of going to college known to my counselor

Workshop Two

Itinerary and Timeline

YOUR PASSPORT TO COLLEGE

Itinerary and Timeline

OBJECTIVE:
Students will gain an understanding of college admission requirements and the step-by-step college application process.

SUMMARY:
Through a passport analogy, students will learn how to meet college admission requirements and how to apply to a four-year institution.

MATERIALS:
AV equipment for PowerPoint presentation (download the file from www.tlpnyc.com/your-passport-to-college), stable internet connection, and two student handouts (My College Requirements and Itinerary and Timeline)

Lesson Vocabulary

Common App n. an undergraduate college admission application that applicants may use to apply to any of more than nine hundred member colleges and universities

early action n. a nonbinding type of admission process that requires students to submit applications earlier, usually between mid-October and early November, than the regular deadline; students are notified by the schools of their decisions early in the admission cycle, typically by January 1

early decision n. an early, binding admission process that allows students to apply to only one school under this type of application; a student accepted as an early decision applicant must attend the college if accepted; students are notified by the schools of their decisions early in the admission cycle

itinerary n. a planned travel route; or a travel document with a planned route

rolling admission n. an admission process that evaluates applicants as their applications are received; schools continue to evaluate applicants until they have filled their slots for the incoming class; decisions are issued in the order in which the applications are received

test-optional n. refers to colleges and universities that do not require applicants to submit the ACT or SAT when applying for admission; they let students decide whether they want to submit scores with their applications and will consider the scores if they are submitted

FACILITATOR NOTE:

Familiarize yourself with the seventeen slides in this lesson, including the embedded video, and page 2 of the student handout prior to facilitation. Make copies of handouts for students.

WARM-UP: PASSPORT ANALOGY

- Begin PowerPoint presentation and stay on **slide #1**. Briefly review the passport analogy from Your Passport to College, Workshop One.
- Present **slide #2**. Tell students that now that they each have a destination and the necessary equipment, today they are going to discuss itinerary and timeline.
- Ask if anyone has heard of an itinerary. If so, ask someone to provide a definition or explaination.
- Tell participants that they will need an itinerary or route to get to their destinations, just as travelers need to have a route to get to their destinations.
- Tell participants they will need to ask themselves, "How do I plan to get to my destination?"
- Tell students that they will also need a timeline.
- Explain that to create a timeline, they need to ask themselves, "When do I need to do what I need to do to get to my destination?"
- Just as if they are going on a trip, they need to do things in a timely manner. For example, you have to show up at the airport on time to catch your flight and you have to make hotel reservations before hotel rooms are sold out. Likewise, tell students that there are timeframes and deadlines by which they need to do things when applying to college.

MAIN ACTIVITY

Part 1: Itinerary

- Present **slide #3: Itinerary**—How do you plan to get to your destination?
- Meet admission requirements: Advise students that they will have to meet college admission requirements. This means that they will have to have taken certain classes in high school before they can apply. Requirements vary by college, but there are some that are pretty common.
- Note to students that meeting admission requirements does not guarantee acceptance.
- Tell students that the types of classes they take in high school matter.
- Let students know that even if they do not yet know which college they would like to attend, it is best to stick to a college prep course of study in high school.
- Review common college admission requirements with students and tell them they should take these classes:

- four years: math
- four years: science with labs
- four years: English
- two years: foreign language (some selective colleges recommend three years)
- two to three years: social science

- Stress to students that colleges like to see that students have challenged themselves based on the classes available to them. The buzz word in admissions circles is "rigor."
- Encourage students to take honors and some AP classes if available, but not to worry if they are unable to do so.

Part 2: Timeline

- Present **slide #4: Timeline**—<u>When</u> do I need to do what I need to do to get to my destination?
- Remind students that to create a timeline, they need to ask themselves, "<u>When</u> do I need to do what I need to do to get to my destination?" Tell them that you will explain the college process in eight steps.
- Present **slide #5: College Application Process** and tell students that you will review each of the eight steps.
- Present **slide #6: Step 1–Make College List.**
  - Review content on slide. Advise students that this is an ongoing process that students should ideally begin in junior year. The list will evolve over time as colleges are added and others are removed. A "final" list should be prepared by the start of senior year.
  - View the explainer video (1:30) included on this slide to introduce the three categories of schools that students should include on their lists.
  - Encourage students to speak to their counselors and other knowledgeable and trusted adults for suggestions to add to their lists.
  - Tell students not to shy away from adding a college to their list because of the cost.
- Present **slide #7: Best-Fit Colleges** and review its content with students.
  - Tell students that you will present them with resources and tips to find their best-fit colleges.
  - Tell students that they are looking to strategically compile their own best-fit list of colleges based on these four factors in addition to their academic records.
  - Stress to students that now is the time to start looking for scholarships. Tell students to look for available institutional scholarship opportunities (those funded by the colleges themselves vs. external scholarships funded by third parties outside of the schools) while researching best-fit schools.
- Present **slide #8: College Search Resources** and review content of slide with students.
- Present **slide #9: Step 2–Determine What's Required.**
  - Explain that once students have their college lists, they will need to review admission

requirements for each of the colleges on their lists. Admission requirements for incoming freshmen can be found on the admission pages of college websites.
- ○ Remind students that they will need to note due dates during this step.
- ○ Distribute the **My College Requirements Worksheet** to students. Explain to students that the back of the worksheet is a great form to use when determining what is required.
- Present **slide #10: Step 3–Submit Test Scores.**
    - ○ Tell students that their test scores should be submitted well before their respective application deadlines.
    - ○ Advise students that they should have discovered the deadlines to submit test scores in Step 2 while determining what's required.
    - ○ Tell students that their test scores will be sent directly from the College Board (the SAT people) or the ACT to their colleges.
    - ○ Advise students that they can elect at no cost to send up to four score reports to schools of their choice at the time they register for either test.
    - ○ Advise students that they will have to go online (www.collegeboard.org or www.act.org) to request that additional scores be sent if they did not request them at the time they registered for their tests.
    - ○ Tell students that there is a fee to send either the ACT or SAT score reports, but that SAT score report waivers are available. Advise students to talk to their counselors ASAP if they need an SAT score report fee waiver. (Note: Score reports are FREE to send if students have a fee waiver to take the ACT.)
- Present **slide #11: Step 4–Gather Necessary Equipment**.
    - ○ Tell students that based on the lists they made in Step 2 when they determined what's required, now is the time to gather the items on those lists.
- Present **slide #12: Step 5–Open Application Accounts.**
- Explain to students that colleges have their own applications and/or they accept a universal application such as the Common App, the Coalition App, or the Universal App.
- Advise students that the Common App is the most popular, as it is accepted by more than nine hundred schools, so you will talk about it for purposes of this presentation.
- Inform students that all colleges have online applications with very few having paper applications, so they will need to be prepared to create application accounts at each of their colleges and/or for the Common App.
- Tell students that they do not have to wait until their senior year to create a Common App account. Let them know they may input all of their data (ex: *demographic profile, education, family history, activities*, etc.) earlier and save it. Doing so reduces their to-do lists in senior year.
- Advise students that there are explainer videos for each of the Common App sections. These YouTube videos are included in the resources section for this workshop. Explain

that the video they are going to watch provides instruction on how to create a Common App account. Play the Common App explainer video (1:38) regarding opening a Common App account.

- Present **slide #13: Step 6–Complete Applications** and review content with participants.
- Present **slide #14: Step 7–Submit Applications** and review content with participants. Advise students there are different types of applicant categories with different deadlines that students need to pay attention to. Categories and deadlines are posted on college admission websites.
- Tell students that while most schools have an application fee ranging anywhere from $25 to $90 per application, there are some schools that do not have application fees. Let them know that many colleges waive application fees. Waiver information, if available, can be found on a college's admission web page.
- Tell students that submitting applications is a situation in which the early bird does get the worm. Stress that scholarship funds are limited and that it is in a student's best interest to submit their application before funds are expended.
- Present **slide #15: Step 8–Wait.**
  - Tell students to use the time after their admission applications are submitted to focus on looking for scholarships.
  - Advise students to keep track of when they should expect to receive decisions from their colleges. Stress the importance of checking their email regularly, as email is the primary way colleges communicate with applicants. Tell them to follow up if they have not received decisions within the published notification timeframes.
- Present **slide #16: Bonus–College Visits.**
- Tell students that not all colleges conduct on-site tours, and they should inquire with the admissions office.
- Provide students with the following tips: take advantage of online 360° tours; and schedule live, virtual tours and information sessions when available.
- Encourage students to follow colleges they're interested in on Instagram, as it's a good way to get a glimpse of campus culture and a look into campus happenings.
- Tell students to look at specific schools and colleges within the institutions they're interested in, such as the School of Business or the College of Allied Health. Those specific schools and colleges may have their own Instagram pages. Also, advise students to peruse websites for specific schools and colleges within the universities on their lists.
- Advise students that some colleges offer "fly-in" programs. Fly-in programs pay for prospective or admitted, high-achieving seniors (usually low-income, first-generation, or students of color) to visit campus for two- or three-day tours. Encourage students to apply for these programs and let them know that there is an article in the resources section that explains fly-in programs in more depth.
- Present **slide #17: Takeaways!**

DISCUSSION QUESTIONS

1. *Am I taking the right classes to meet college admission requirements?*
2. *What are my personal preferences in a college?*

CLOSING

- I will use the following tools to help organize my college application timeline and keep track of important deadlines: _____.
- People that I can ask for letters of recommendation include _____.

EXTENSION ACTIVITY

- Tell students to start thinking about their preferences in a college.
- Ask juniors to begin compiling their lists of best-fit colleges.

RESOURCES

- www.commonapp.org/ready: Written resources designed to help students complete the Common App
- www.youtube.com/@CommonAppMedia: The Common App YouTube channel is filled with explainer videos for each section of the application
- https://youtu.be/1u3BVR24ffE: How to Choose the Perfect College for You is a video that reviews things to consider when selecting a good-fit college
- https://youtu.be/T0wwsKViWfc: How to Build Your College List is a video resource that explains reach, safety, and target schools
- www.usnews.com/education/best-colleges/articles/2017-05-01/diversity-fly-in-programs-make-campus-visits-accessible: Diversity Fly-in Programs Make Campus Visits Accessible
- www.collegeessayguy.com/matchlighters: Matchlighters Scholarship offers FREE college application counseling for high-achieving, low-income students from experienced college counselors (note: students are often encouraged to apply by August)

My College Requirements Worksheet

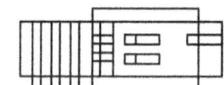

Staying organized and understanding what you need to fill out in the application is crucial. But, because each college has its own specific requirements, it can seem like a lot to keep track of.

Use this worksheet to collect the requirements of the colleges on your list. This way you have all the information in one place when you need it. We've included space for 4 colleges, but if you have more you want to add, just copy and paste the last page!

Here is where you can find colleges' requirements in the application:

College Search tab
Select a college from the list to open their requirements. You can also use the "more info" icon for links to other helpful resources.

My Colleges tab
Each college's "College Information" page contains all their specific requirements.

Requirements Grid
This PDF lists all colleges that use Common App and their requirements. You can access this document on your Dashboard, in College Search, or in the Solutions Center.

Writing Requirements by college
This FAQ lists out all the Common App colleges and their writing questions. You can find it in our Solutions Center at appsupport.commonapp.org

Property of Common App, Inc. | © 2019 Common App, Inc. | commonapp.org

College Name:

_____

Deadline: _____

Application Fee: _____

Personal Essay:
☐ Yes ☐ Optional

Courses & Grades:
☐ Yes ☐ No

Supplements:
☐ Portfolio
☐ Writing Supplement

Testing Policy:
☐ SAT/ACT Tests Used
☐ Always Required
☐ Sometimes Required
☐ Never Required
☐ Flexible
☐ Ignored

Writing Questions:
☐ Yes
☐ No
☐ Additional Information

Recommendations:
Teacher Evaluations:
____ Required   ____ Optional

Other Evaluations:
____ Required   ____ Optional

Types Accepted:
☐ Arts Teacher
☐ Clergy
☐ Coach
☐ College Access Counselor
☐ Employer
☐ Family Member
☐ Peer
☐ Other

Property of Common App, Inc. | © 2019 Common App, Inc. | commonapp.org

NAME:

WORKSHOP TWO: ITINERARY AND TIMELINE

Itinerary—I must do the following to get to my college destination:

- Meet _____ requirements
- Select appropriate _____
    - _____ Math
    - _____ Science
    - _____ English
    - _____ Foreign Language
    - _____ Social Science

Eight-Step College Application Process:

(1) _____
(2) _____
(3) _____
(4) _____
(5) _____
(6) _____
(7) _____
(8) _____

My college list should include schools in each of the following categories:

R_____
T_____
S_____

I can use the following search resources to compile my college list:

- www._____.org
- www._____.com

Common App:

- I opened my account on: _____
- My Common App password: _____

Test Scores—ACT and SAT:
- I can register for the ACT here: www._____.org
- I can register for the SAT here: www._____.org

Stay abreast of testing matters with Instagram:
- @actstudent
- @collegeboard

QUESTIONS

1. *Am I taking the right classes to meet college admission requirements? If not, I will arrange to meet with my counselor ASAP.*

PLANNING AHEAD

- I will use the following tools (ex: *paper planner, spreadsheet, calendar app,* etc.) to help organize my college application timeline and keep track of important deadlines: _____
_____
_____

- People whom I can ask for letters of recommendation include: _____
_____
_____
_____
_____

EXERCISES

List your personal preferences in a college. Write them here.
_____
_____
_____
_____
_____
_____
_____
_____

Begin compiling your list of best-fit colleges. Write them here.

NOTES

ANSWERS

WORKSHOP TWO: ITINERARY AND TIMELINE

Itinerary—I must do the following to get to my college destination:
- Meet _____admission_____ requirements
- Select appropriate _____high school classes_____
    - __4__ Math
    - __4__ Science
    - __4__ English
    - __2__ Foreign Language
    - __2 or 3__ Social Science

Eight-Step College Application Process:
(1) _____Make a college list_____
(2) _____Determine what's required_____
(3) _____Submit test scores_____
(4) _____Gather necessary equipment_____
(5) _____Open application account_____
(6) _____Complete applications_____
(7) _____Submit applications_____
(8) _____Wait_____

My college list should include schools in each of the following categories:

R_____Reach_____
T_____Target_____
S_____Safety_____

I can use the following search resources to compile my college list:
- www._____bigfuture.collegeboard_____.org
- www._____collegesimply_____.com

Test Scores—ACT and SAT:
- I can register for the ACT here: www._____act_____.org
- I can register for the SAT here: www._____collegeboard_____.org

Slide #1

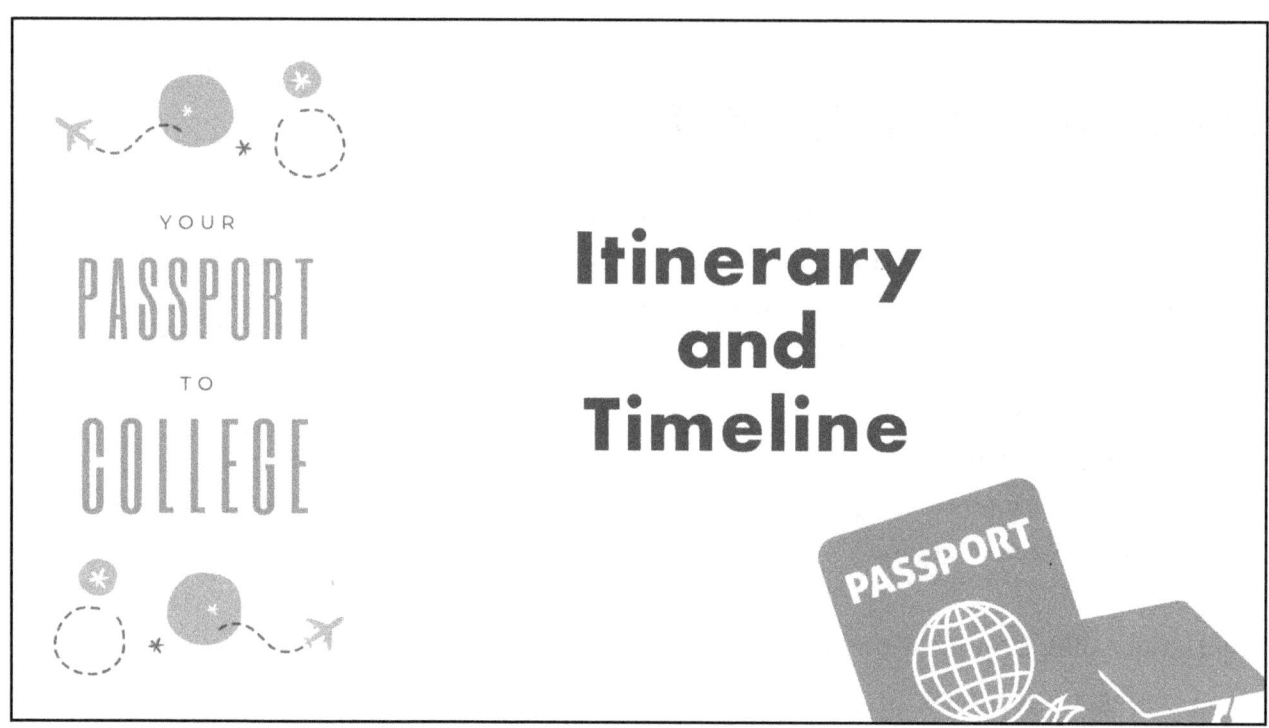

Slide #2

Review

Destination—Where do you want to go?

Equipment—What will you need to get there?

Route or Itinerary—How do you want to get there?

Timeline—When do you want to get there?

Slide #3

Itinerary

How do you get to your destination?

- Meet admission requirements
- Select appropriate high school classes

Common college admission requirements:
- Math—four years
- Science (with labs)—four years
- English—four years
- Foreign Language—two years
- Social Science—two to three years

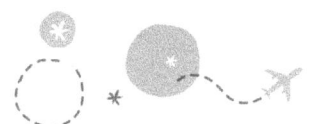

Slide #4

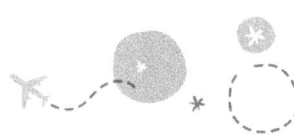

Timeline

When do you need to do what you need to do to get to your destination?

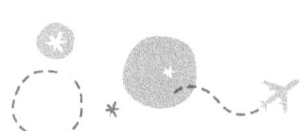

Slide #5

Eight-Step College Application Process

- Step 1—Make college list
- Step 2—Determine what's required
- Step 3—Submit test scores
- Step 4—Gather necessary equipment
- Step 5—Open application accounts
- Step 6—Complete applications
- Step 7—Submit applications
- Step 8—Wait

Slide #6

Timeline

Step 1: Make College List

When?
Ongoing—ideally, students should have a final list at the beginning of senior year

Reach—Test scores and GPA fall slightly below those of the current freshman class and the rest of the academic record is solid

Target—Test scores and GPA match those of the current freshman class

Safety—Test scores and GPA exceed those of the current freshman class

Slide #7

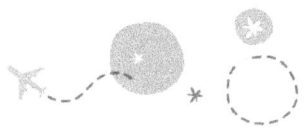
Best-Fit Colleges

- Academics—Are my first and second choice majors available?

- Location—Is the school located somewhere I am willing to live for four years?

- Cost—Is this college affordable considering grants and scholarships?

- Preferences—What do I consider important? Examples: Class size? Urban setting? College town? Division I sports? Proximity to home? Available clubs?

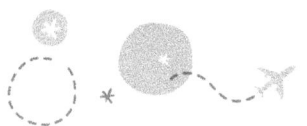

Slide #8

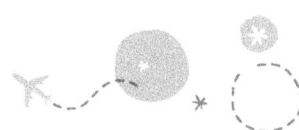
College Search Resources

- www.bigfuture.collegeboard.org—Search tool to help you find the right school for YOU

- www.collegesimply.com—Tool that helps find colleges that you may get into based on your GPA and SAT or ACT score

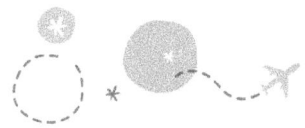

Slide #9

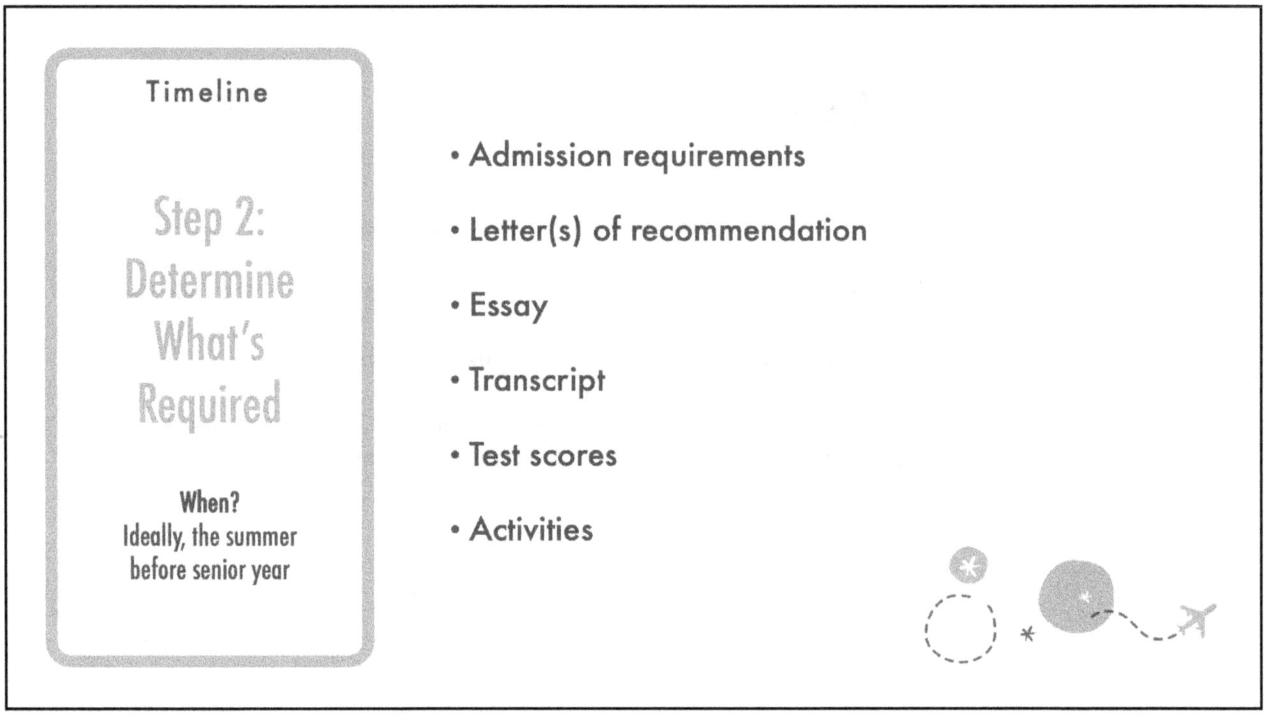

Timeline

Step 2: Determine What's Required

When?
Ideally, the summer before senior year

- Admission requirements
- Letter(s) of recommendation
- Essay
- Transcript
- Test scores
- Activities

Slide #10

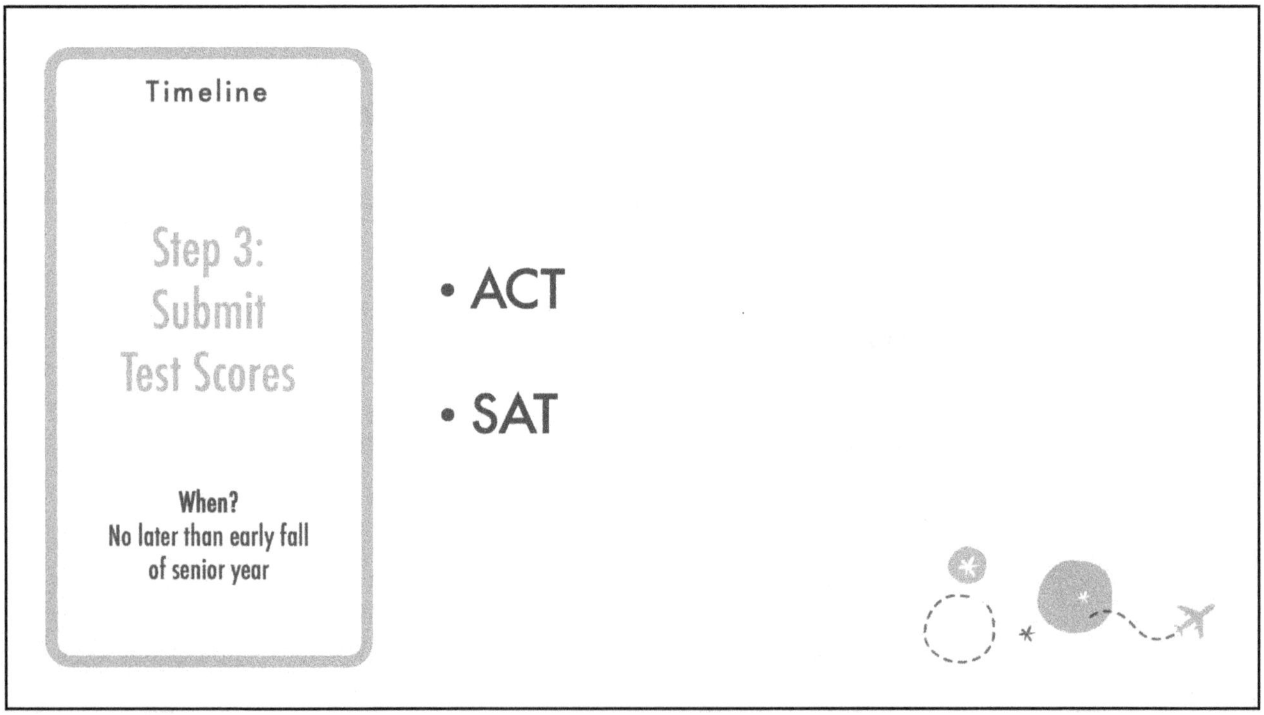

Timeline

Step 3: Submit Test Scores

When?
No later than early fall of senior year

- ACT
- SAT

Slide #11

Timeline

Step 4:
Gather
Necessary
Equipment

When?
Ideally, the summer
before senior year

- Letter(s) of recommendation
- Essay
- Transcript
- Test scores
- Activities
- Portfolio

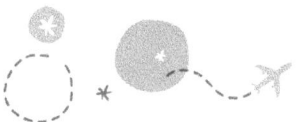

Slide #12

Timeline

Step 5:
Open
Application
Accounts

When?
Colleges typically open their
application portals on August 1 or
August 15, but some as early as
July 1 and as late as September 1

- Common App—You may open an account any time and save it until your senior year
- Passwords—You will not remember all of them, so write them down

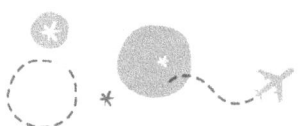

Slide #13

Timeline

**Step 6:
Complete
Applications**

When?
Before deadlines—
earlier is better

- Fee waivers—Many colleges offer application fee waivers. Qualifications and instructions on how to obtain waivers, if available, can be found on each college's website.

- Make it a date!—Completing applications takes time. Schedule one-to-two-hour increments to work on completing applications. They do not have to be finished in one sitting.

Slide #14

Timeline

**Step 7:
Submit
Applications**

When?
The sooner the better—the goal is to have all applications submitted by November 1, unless there is an early priority deadline

Colleges often have different due dates based on the category of application. Get familiar with the following categories. Each college explains its categories on its website.

- Priority
- Regular
- Early Action
- Early Decision

Colleges will also specify the timeframes during which they will release their admissions decisions. Some colleges have rolling admission instead.

Slide #15

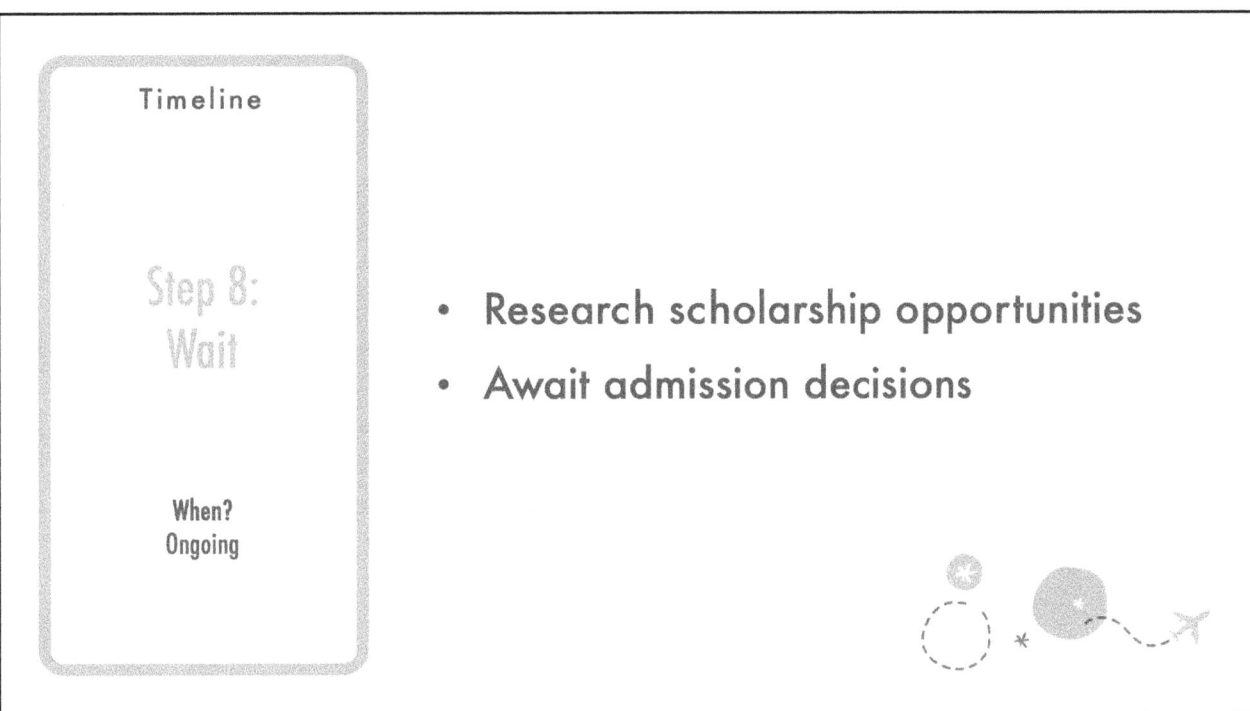

Slide #16

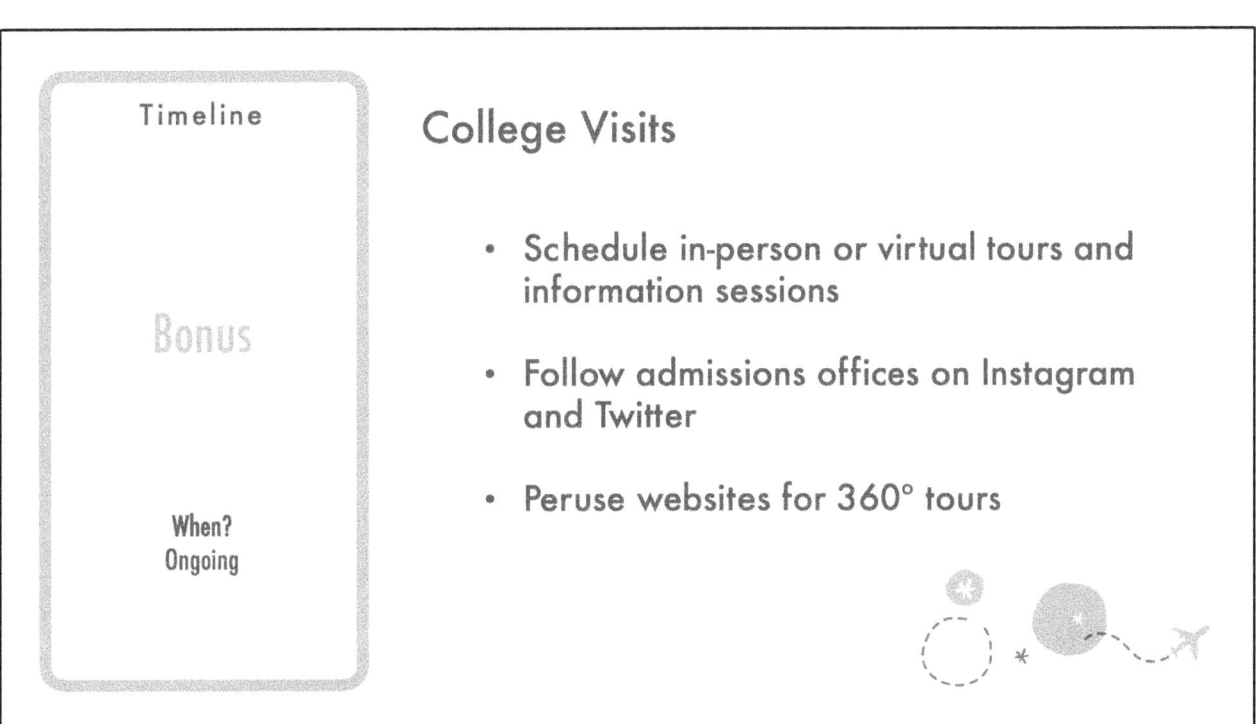

Slide #17

Workshop Three

College Essays, Part 1

YOUR PASSPORT TO COLLEGE

College Essays, Part 1

OBJECTIVE:
Students examine the Common App essay prompts, select their prompts, and learn what colleges are looking for in a well-written, responsive essay.

SUMMARY:
Through brainstorming exercises and examining model essays, students will learn, over the course of two workshops, how to select a meaningful essay topic, and they will learn the dos and don'ts of crafting a well-written essay.

MATERIALS:
AV equipment for PowerPoint presentation (download the file from www.tlpnyc.com/your-passport-to-college), stable internet connection, notebook or blank paper for brainstorming exercises, two student handouts (The Values Exercise and College Essays, Parts 1 and 2), and pens or pencils

Lesson Vocabulary

active voice n. a sentence in which the subject performs the action denoted by the verb

cliché n. an overused expression or idea that has lost its original meaning or effect, even to the point of being trite or irritating

hook n. the opening sentence of an essay designed to engage the reading audience; it draws the audience into the essay and sparks the audience's curiosity

passive voice n. a sentence in which the subject is not active but is, instead, being acted upon by the verb

FACILITATOR NOTE:
Familiarize yourself with the twelve slides in this lesson, prior to facilitation. Make copies of handouts for students.

WARM-UP: FIVE-PARAGRAPH ESSAY COMPARISON

- Ask students if they know how to write a traditional five-paragraph essay. Wait for their responses.
- Follow-up by telling them that it does not matter if they know how to or not because the college application essay is not the five-paragraph essay.
- Let students know that the college application is a different animal altogether. It is written in a more casual style (tone, voice, and structure), but good grammar is still required.
- Tell students that this will be the first of two sessions that they will have to learn about and work on the college application essay.

MAIN ACTIVITY

Part 1: Brainstorming Exercises

- Begin PowerPoint presentation. Stay on **slide #1**. Let students know that they are going to complete three brainstorming exercises.
- Present **slide #2**:
    - Brainstorming Exercise #1: "I love _____." Give students three to four minutes to write down all of the things that they love. Inform students that their lists can include people, places, things, events, or activities. It can be anything that they love. Let students know that their lists will not be shared.
    - Brainstorming Exercise #2: "I know _____." Now tell students that they will create lists of things that they know for sure or are good at. Give participants three to four minutes to make their lists. Students will keep their lists to themselves.
- Let students know that it is now time for their last brainstorming exercise.
- Brainstorming Exercise #3: Values. Proceed to **slide #3** and distribute **The Values Exercise** worksheet to each student.
    - Instruct students to select their ten most important values. Give them three to four minutes to complete this task.
    - Next, ask students to identify their top five values from their lists of ten. Give them one to two minutes to complete this task.
    - Now ask students to select their top three values from their list of five. Give them one minute.
    - Last, ask students to select the number one value on their lists.
- Advise students to keep all of their lists and top values in mind while choosing their Common App essay prompt. Items on their lists may give them inspiration or trigger a memory about something or someone that would make for a great essay topic.
- Give students about one minute to look over all three of their brainstorming exercises.
- Tell students that not all colleges that accept the Common App require the essay. This is something that students should have noticed and noted during Step 2 (Determine What's Required) of the college application process.

Part 2: Common App Prompts

- Present **slide #4: Common App Prompts**. Let students know that each year the Common App publishes a list of prompts. There are seven of them.
- Provide students a few minutes to read through the prompts.
- Present **slides #5-11** (**Prompt #1** to **Prompt #7**) and review the content of each slide (approx. three minutes/slide) before advancing to the next slide.
- Present **slide #12: Takeaways!**

DISCUSSION QUESTION

1. *What life event, life experience, or ordinary happening(s) can I use to craft an interesting personal story to tell?*

CLOSING

- I can ask the following person or people to help me with my Common App essay _____.

EXTENSION ACTIVITY

- Advise students to keep a log or to jot down events or experiences that would make for good essay topics.

RESOURCES

- https://blog.collegevine.com/how-to-write-the-common-application-essays-2022-2023/: How to Write the Common Application Essays 2022–2023
- https://youtu.be/AmZR0Y_GxNQ: 3 Stupid Essay Mistakes on the Common Application—Don't Do These!
- https://youtu.be/ys25IoqNHNk: Crush the Common Application Essay! 8 Tips

NAME: _____

THE VALUES EXERCISE

How it works: Place a check mark beside your Top 10 values.

- ○ community
- ○ inspiration
- ○ money
- ○ intellectual
- ○ status
- ○ financial gain
- ○ laughter
- ○ serenity
- ○ physical challenge
- ○ responsibility
- ○ competition
- ○ career
- ○ fame
- ○ working with others
- ○ freedom
- ○ security
- ○ strength
- ○ self-control
- ○ hunger
- ○ personal development
- ○ trust
- ○ faith
- ○ involvement
- ○ adventure
- ○ vulnerability
- ○ adaptability
- ○ friendship
- ○ excellence
- ○ job tranquility
- ○ power
- ○ passion
- ○ cooperation
- ○ affection
- ○ wisdom
- ○ knowledge

- ○ self-expression
- ○ stability
- ○ art
- ○ autonomy
- ○ risk
- ○ balance
- ○ self-discipline
- ○ courage
- ○ family
- ○ empathy
- ○ working alone
- ○ humility
- ○ efficiency
- ○ intensity
- ○ health and fitness
- ○ meaningful work
- ○ my country
- ○ music
- ○ truth
- ○ resourcefulness
- ○ challenges
- ○ commitment
- ○ leadership
- ○ helping others
- ○ influence
- ○ wit
- ○ success
- ○ patience
- ○ listening
- ○ diversity
- ○ love
- ○ fast-paced work
- ○ nutrition
- ○ competence
- ○ practicality

- ○ beauty
- ○ ecological awareness
- ○ quality relationships
- ○ travel
- ○ decisiveness
- ○ curiosity
- ○ spirituality
- ○ loyalty
- ○ honesty
- ○ independence
- ○ supervising others
- ○ recognition
- ○ accountability
- ○ democracy
- ○ close relationships
- ○ religion
- ○ respect
- ○ bravery
- ○ communication
- ○ change and variety
- ○ compassion
- ○ nature
- ○ growth
- ○ expertise
- ○ order
- ○ privacy
- ○ creativity
- ○ excitement
- ○ collaboration
- ○ social change
- ○ _____
- ○ _____
- ○ _____
- ○ _____
- ○ _____

Excerpted from College Essay Essentials: A Step-by-Step Guide to Writing a Successful College Admissions Essay
www.collegeessayguy.com | help@collegeessayguy.com

NAME: _____

WORKSHOPS THREE AND FOUR: COLLEGE ESSAYS, PARTS 1 AND 2

BRAINSTORMING EXERCISES

#1—"I love..."
Take a few minutes to complete this sentence:
I love _____
_____
_____
_____.

Write down all of the things that you love. Your list may include people, places, things, events, or activities.

#2—"I know..."
Take a few minutes to complete this sentence:
I know _____
_____
_____
_____.

Write down all of the things that you know for sure and/or the things that you are good at.

#3—Values
Take a few minutes to select your top ten values from the list provided. Then select your top five from your ten. Next, select your top three from your remaining list. Finally, select your top value.

Top Ten Values	Top Five Values	Top Three Values	My Top Value
1.	1.	1.	
2.	2.	2.	
3.	3.	3.	
4.	4.		
5.	5.		
6.			
7.			
8.			
9.			
10.			

My Favorite Common App Prompt

Circle your top two choices:

#1—Share Your Story

#2—Learn from Obstacles

#3—Challenging a Belief

#4—Solving a Problem

#5—Personal Growth and Maturity

#6—Passion—What Captivates You?

#7—Your Choice

Essay Dos

- Craft an engaging _____.
- Use _____ voice.
- _____ versus tell.
- Use _____ verbs.
- Be _____.
- Avoid overuse of _____ and _____.
- Use _____ sentence length and structure.
- Avoid _____.
- Use your _____ voice.

Essay Don'ts

- Write an _____.
- Use _____ voice.
- T_____
- Force _____.
- Repeat your _____.
- Use _____ topics.
- Use _____.

A great online thesaurus: www._____.com

QUESTIONS

1. Do I have anything on the lists from my brainstorming exercises that I can use to develop an engaging essay topic?

PLANNING AHEAD

I can ask the following person or people to help me with my Common App essay: _____
_____
_____
_____

EXERCISES

Use this space to jot down events or experiences that would make good essay topics.

NOTES

ANSWERS

WORKSHOPS THREE AND FOUR: COLLEGE ESSAYS, PARTS 1 AND 2

Essay Dos
- Craft an engaging _____hook_____.
- Use _____active_____ voice.
- _____Show_____ versus tell.
- Use _____descriptive_____ verbs.
- Be _____specific_____.
- Avoid overuse of _____"I"_____ and _____"to be" verbs_____.
- Use _____varied_____ sentence length and structure.
- Avoid _____repetition_____.
- Use your _____authentic_____ voice.

Essay Don'ts
- Write an _____autobiography_____.
- Use _____passive_____ voice.
- T_____Tell_____
- Force _____humor_____.
- Repeat your _____resume_____.
- Use _____overused_____ topics.
- Use _____clichés_____.

A great online thesaurus: www._____wordhippo_____.com

Slide #1

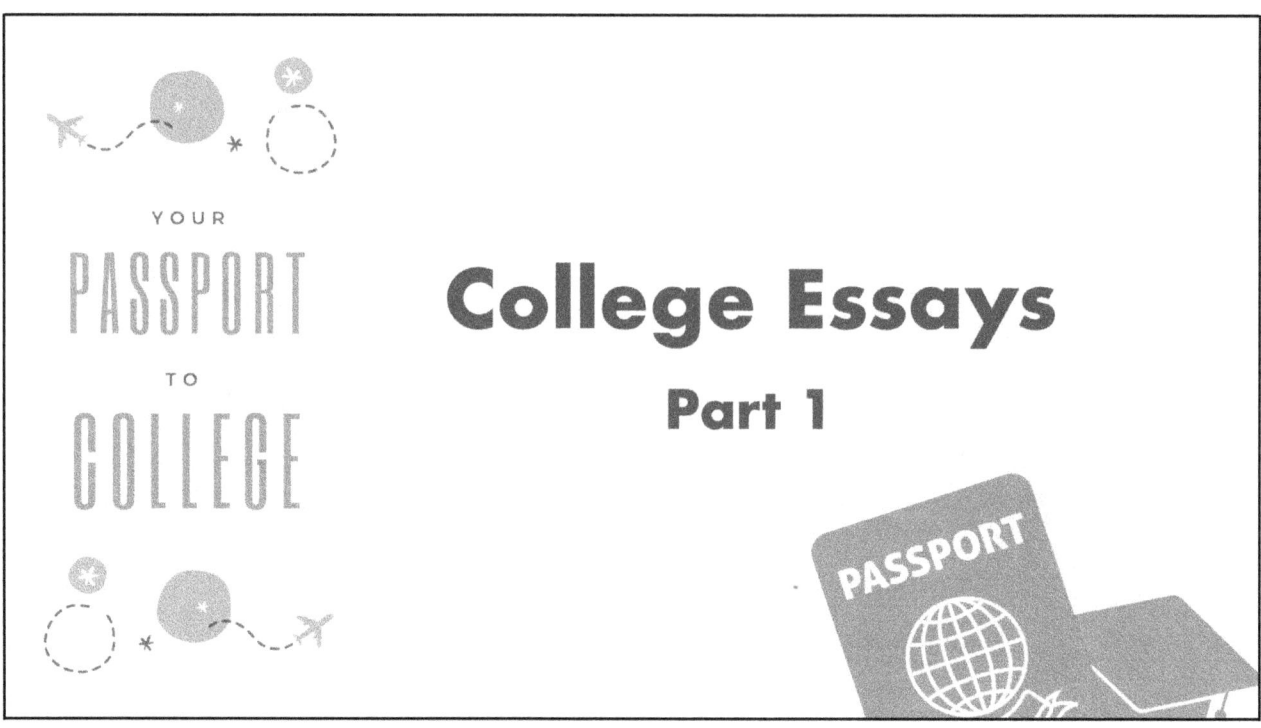

Slide #2

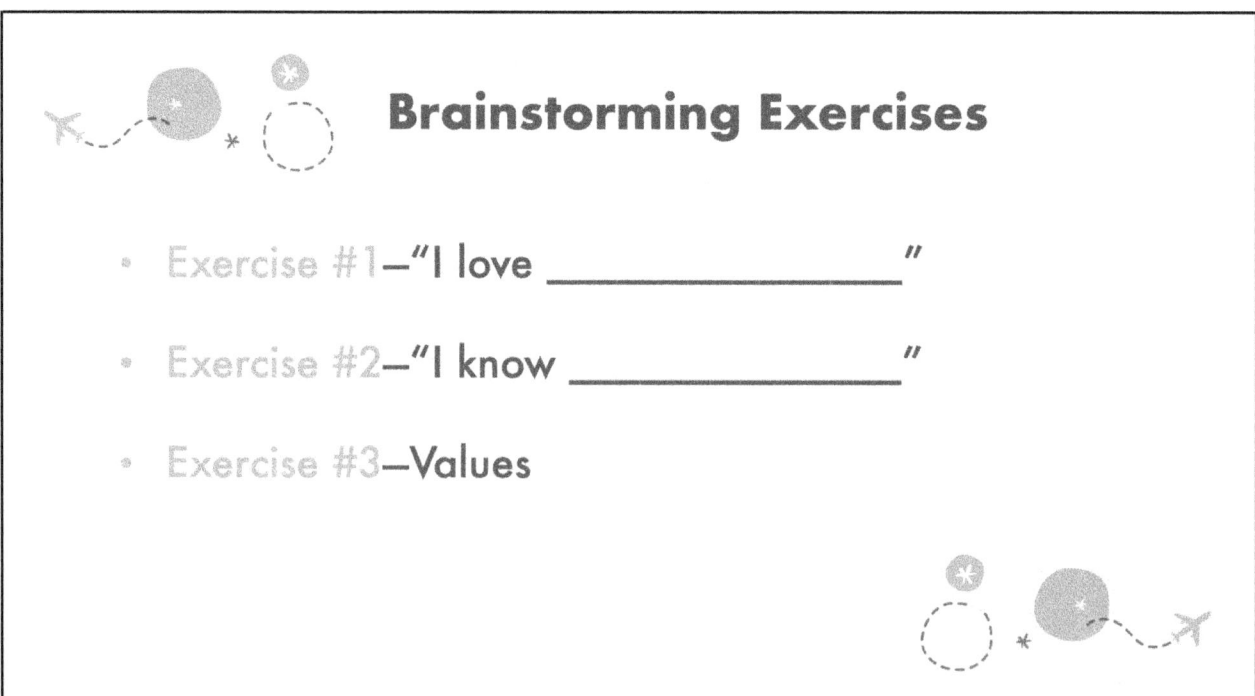

Slide #3

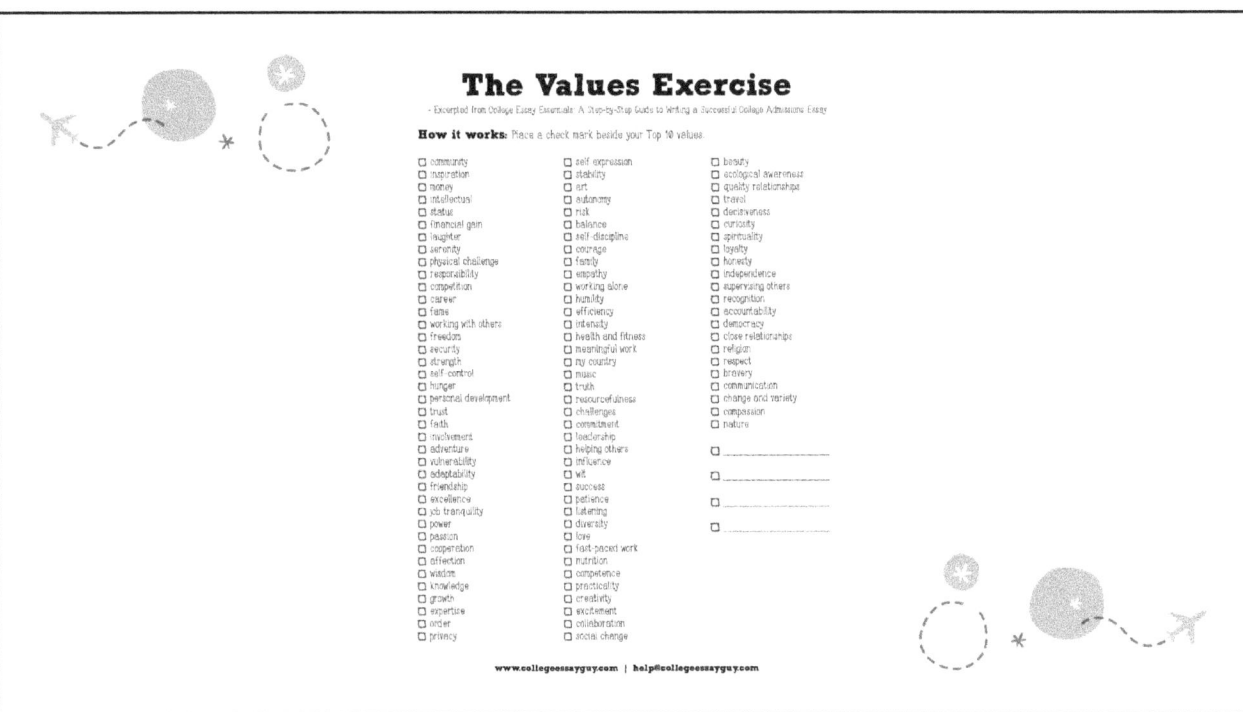

Slide #4

Common App Prompts—Overview

1. Some students have a background, identity, interest, or talent that is so meaningful they believe their application would be incomplete without it. If this sounds like you, then please share your story.

2. The lessons we take from obstacles we encounter can be fundamental to later success. Recount a time when you faced a challenge, setback, or failure. How did it affect you, and what did you learn from the experience?

3. Reflect on a time when you questioned or challenged a belief or idea. What prompted your thinking? What was the outcome?

4. Describe a problem you've solved or a problem you'd like to solve. It can be an intellectual challenge, a research query, an ethical dilemma—anything that is of personal importance, no matter the scale. Explain its significance to you and what steps you took or could take to identify a solution.

5. Discuss an accomplishment, event, or realization that sparked a period of personal growth and a new understanding of yourself or others.

6. Describe a topic, idea, or concept you find so engaging that it makes you lose all track of time. Why does it captivate you? What or who do you turn to when you want to learn more?

7. Share an essay on any topic of your choice. It can be one you've already written, one that responds to a different prompt, or one of your own design.

Slide #5

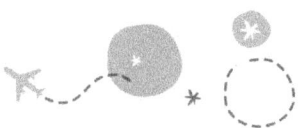

Prompt #1—Share Your Story

Some students have a background, identity, interest, or talent that is so meaningful they believe their application would be incomplete without it. If this sounds like you, then please share your story.

- Show how your background has shaped you. Can you learn and grow from your experiences?
- Do not rehash your resume
- Can be anything from a major milestone to an aha moment
- Admissions officers want to feel connected to you

Slide #6

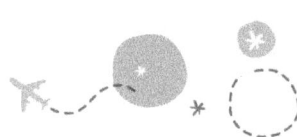

Prompt #2—Learn from Obstacles

The lessons we take from obstacles we encounter can be fundamental to later success. Recount a time when you faced a challenge, setback, or failure. How did it affect you, and what did you learn from the experience?

- Show how you handle difficult situations
- Show that you are able to learn from your mistakes
- A change in perspective is important
- Admissions officers want to know that you can face challenges without giving up

Slide #7

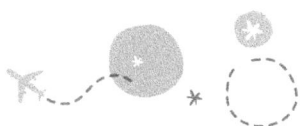

Prompt #3—Challenging a Belief

Reflect on a time when you questioned or challenged a belief or idea. What prompted your thinking? What was the outcome?

- Two options: you've questioned a person or group; or something caused you to reconsider a belief of your own
- Relevance and specificity are required
- Conflict + resulting action must be included
- Admissions officers want to know what you value, whether you are willing to stand up for what you believe, and whether you are open-minded

Slide #8

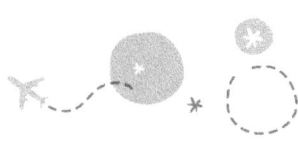

Prompt #4—Solving a Problem

Describe a problem you've solved or a problem you'd like to solve. It can be an intellectual challenge, a research query, an ethical dilemma—anything that is of personal importance, no matter the scale. Explain its significance to you and what steps you took or could take to identify a solution.

- Explain significance of the problem
- Lets admissions officers know what you care about
- Opportunity to demonstrate maturity and perseverance
- Admissions officers want to know how you think and what makes you tick

Slide #9

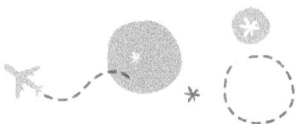

Prompt #5—Personal Growth and Maturity

Discuss an accomplishment, event, or realization that sparked a period of personal growth and a new understanding of yourself or others.

- Explain how this event changed or enriched your understanding of yourself or other people
- Admissions officers want to know when and how you have grown as a person

Slide #10

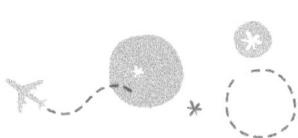

Prompt #6—Passion—What Captivates You?

Describe a topic, idea, or concept you find so engaging that it makes you lose all track of time. Why does it captivate you? What or who do you turn to when you want to learn more?

- Describe something that you are intellectually passionate about
- Include in detail how you have pursued furthering your own knowledge of the topic
- Admissions officers want to know that you have a genuine love for the pursuit of knowledge and that you are self-motivated and resourceful

Slide #11

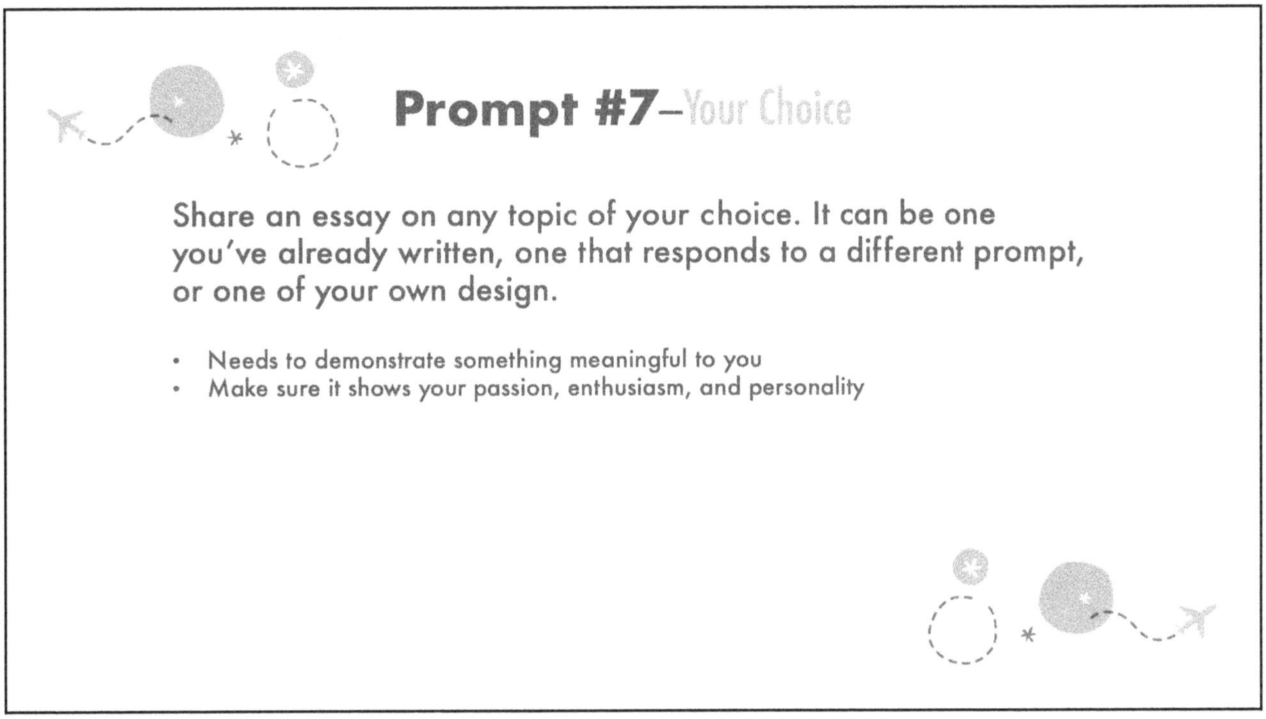

Prompt #7—Your Choice

Share an essay on any topic of your choice. It can be one you've already written, one that responds to a different prompt, or one of your own design.

- Needs to demonstrate something meaningful to you
- Make sure it shows your passion, enthusiasm, and personality

Slide #12

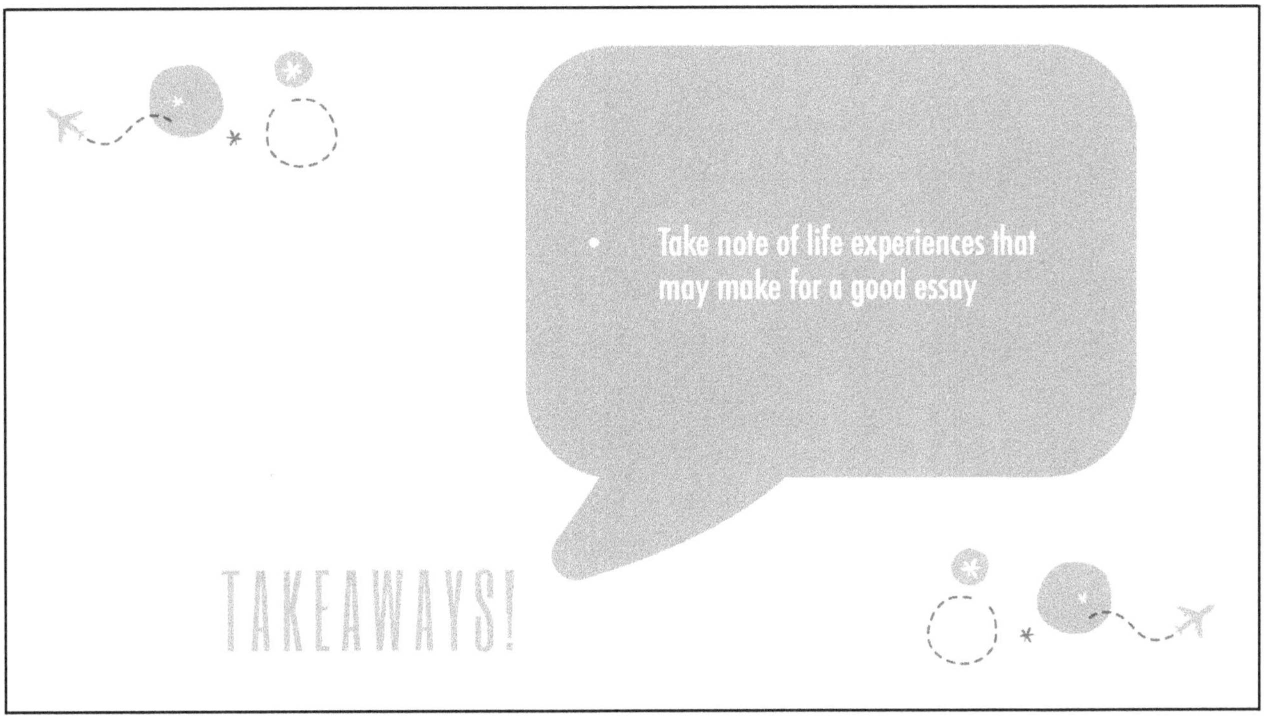

TAKEAWAYS!

- Take note of life experiences that may make for a good essay

Workshop Four

College Essays, Part 2

YOUR PASSPORT TO COLLEGE

College Essays, Part 2

OBJECTIVE:
Students will learn essay strategies, structures, and best practice dos and don'ts for writing a Common App essay.

SUMMARY:
Students will implement strategies and best practice dos and don'ts to write a Common App essay.

MATERIALS:
AV equipment for PowerPoint presentation (download the file from www.tlpnyc.com/your-passport-to-college) and stable internet connection

Lesson Vocabulary

active voice n. a sentence in which the subject performs the action denoted by the verb

cliché n. an overused expression or idea that has lost its original meaning or effect, even to the point of being trite or irritating

Common App n. an undergraduate college admission application that applicants may use to apply to any of more than 900 member colleges and universities

passive voice n. a sentence in which the subject is not active but is, instead, being acted upon by the verb

FACILITATOR NOTE:
Familiarize yourself with the twelve slides in this lesson, including the embedded video, prior to facilitation. Make copies of handouts for students.

WARM-UP: PASSPORT ANALOGY

- Begin PowerPoint presentation. Stay on **slide #1** during the warm-up.
- Inform participants that this is the second part of the Common App essay workshop.
- Remind students that there are seven prompts from which to choose for the Common App. (Prompts may be found at www.commonapp.org under the Apply to College tab.)
- Advise students that the essay is of greater importance during the application cycle, as many colleges and universities have waived standardized test scores (ACT or SAT) as an admission requirement in light of COVID-19.
- Stress that good writing takes time and the importance of students not waiting until the last minute to begin their essays.

# MAIN ACTIVITY (INCLUDES A 12:29-MINUTE VIDEO)

- Present **slide #2: Common App Prompts** and read each of the prompts aloud. This will be a review.
- Tell students that you are going to share three sample essays.
- Present **slide #3: Sample Essay #1** and ask students to follow along as you read aloud.
- When you are finished reading, ask participants to tell which prompt they believe the student answers. (Correct answer: Prompt #3—Solving a Problem.)
- Inform students that this is a good essay.
- Ask students to tell what makes it a good essay. Answers will vary.
- Tell students that it is a good first-draft essay because it answers the three parts of the prompt—describes a problem, tells the personal significance of the problem, and identifies steps taken for a solution. It also has a pretty interesting first sentence and the reader learns something significant about the author through the essay.
- Inform participants that the author sought feedback from a trusted adult before she made revisions and incorporated that feedback in her second draft.
- Advise students that they are now going to hear the revised version of this essay. Proceed to **slide #4: Revised Sample Essay #1** and ask students to follow along as you read aloud.
- Ask students if they notice any changes from the original essay. Wait for responses. Answers will vary.
- Tell students that these are some of the differences: the revision is more engaging and it tells a story; the first sentence in the revision better captures the reader's attention; the revision includes more details and incorporates dialogue, which makes it more interesting.
- Inform students that they will review one last sample essay. It was written a few years ago and is widely available on the internet. The student uses an ordinary experience and writes a masterful essay.
- Present **slide #5: Sample Essay #2** and ask students to follow along as you read aloud.
- When you are finished reading, ask participants to tell which prompt they believe the student answered. (Correct answer: Prompt #1—Share Your Story.)
- Ask students what makes this an outstanding essay? Answers will vary.
- Inform students that this is an excellent essay because the student tells a story while painting a vivid picture with strong verbs; shows how she takes the ordinary, shopping at a warehouse store, to reveal a personal characteristic (intellectual curiosity); makes the connection between the curiosity she developed at Costco to her intellectual endeavors in high school; and subtly weaves in her analytical prowess (reference to Old Hickory).
- Present **slide #6: Sample Essay #2—Strong Verbs.**
- Tell students that you are going to examine the strong verbs the student used in the Costco essay. Read the highlighted verbs aloud to students and tell them that strong, specific verbs help paint a vivid picture.

- Ask students if they can visualize the writer inside Costco. There may be some discussion.
- Proceed to **slide #7: Types of Essays**. Tell students that there are two general structures of college application essays, narrative and collage, and note that one is not better than the other. Review the content of this slide.
- Ask students whether the first sample (swimming essay) is narrative or collage. (Correct answer: narrative.)
- Ask students whether the second sample essay (Costco) has a narrative or collage structure. (Correct answer: collage.)
- Present **slide #8: Best Practice Dos and Don'ts** and review the content as follows:
    ○ Craft an engaging hook: The purpose is to capture the reader's attention.
    ○ Use active voice: It conveys a strong, clear tone (ex: *The cashier counted the money*). Tell students there is a resource included with this workshop that explains the difference between active versus passive voices.
    ○ Show: Use description and action to help the reader experience the story; do not simply tell.
    ○ Use strong verbs: They are specific and descriptive (ex: *the Costco essay*).
    ○ Be specific: Details matter, but keep the 650-word limit in mind.
    ○ Avoid overuse of "I" and "to be" verbs: To be verbs: am, is, was, were, be, being, and been.
    ○ Use varied sentence length and structure: It makes for more interesting reading.
    ○ Avoid repetition: Use a thesaurus (www.wordhippo.com), but maintain your voice.
    ○ Use your authentic voice: The essay should sound like the writer's voice, and the reader should feel the presence of the writer.
    ○ Do not write an autobiography: This is not the time to tell your whole life story.
    ○ Do not use the passive voice: Generally makes for flat and uninteresting writing.
    ○ Do not "tell": The author summarizes or uses exposition to tell what happens.
    ○ Do not force humor: Humor is OK, but do not try to be funny.
    ○ Do not repeat your resume: Do not rehash information contained elsewhere in your application.
    ○ Do not use overused topics: You don't want to lose your reader's attention, as each reader typically reads hundreds of essays.
    ○ Do not use clichés: They show a lack of original thought and creativity.
- Present **slide #9: Topics to Avoid**. Explain that these topics are overused and/or they do not allow students opportunities to provide much insight into who they are. Use the following to present the slide content:
    ○ The Trip: Avoid writing about a trip that broadened your horizons, gave you a new perspective, increased empathy, or allowed you to learn about your cultural heritage. It's too cliché.

- My Favorite Things: Classic fluff—this topic is perceived as trivial and superficial.
- Miss America: Avoid too general of a response to a topic. Ex: *I think world peace is the most important issue facing us today* is too broad of a response to Prompt #3 (Solving a Problem).
- Pet Death: Avoid anything along the lines of *As I watched Button's life ebb away, I came to value the important things in the world.*
- Your "Jock" Story: This is a formula to avoid: Through [fill in activity], I have learned [noble value A], [high platitude B], and [great lesson C]. Ex: *Through wrestling, I have learned to set goals, to go all out, and to work with other people.*
- The 3 Ds—discipline, determination, and diversity: These qualities can be gleaned from elsewhere in your application.

• Present **slide #10: 5 College Essays That Suck** and tell students that they will watch a video (12:29) that discusses five essay topics that they should avoid. Some of it will sound familiar to them.

• Present **slide #11: General Writing Process** and review the content.
- Prewrite: Tell students to review prompts and make sure students understand what's being asked by each prompt.
- Brainstorm: Encourage students to use the lists from the brainstorming exercises in Part 1 of this workshop to generate topic ideas. Let students know that it is OK to keep brainstorming if they are not inspired by anything on their current lists. Tell students that this step often takes the longest. It is OK for students to change prompts if they find they are having a hard time coming up with an engaging topic.
- Draft: Let students know that now they may begin writing. They should read what's been written as they go along. Write some more. Read what has been written. Write some more. Students continue this cycle until they have written everything they want to say on the topic.
- Sit: Tell students that ideally they should let their drafts sit for at least one day prior to making revisions.
- Revise: Tell students they should read their drafts aloud during this stage. This is the stage to rearrange words and sentences, to take out or add parts, and to replace overused or unclear words.
- Solicit: Encourage students to ask a trusted adult to review and provide feedback on their first drafts.
- Revise: Tell students to repeat this stage.
- Solicit: Advise students to repeat this stage as many times as necessary. After the last draft has been deemed final, students should move to the next stage.
- Polish: Inform students that this is the editing and proofreading stage. Students should

closely review for complete sentences, and check spelling and usage (capitalization and punctuation). There is no room for error.
- ○ Solicit: Advise students that they should ask someone to review their essays one last time for spelling, grammar, and usage errors.
- Present **slide #12: Takeaways!**

DISCUSSION QUESTIONS

1. *Which two essay prompts do I like best?*
2. *Do I have anything on the lists from my brainstorming exercises that I can use to develop an engaging essay topic?*

CLOSING

- People that can help with proofing my essay include _____.

EXTENSION ACTIVITY

- Tell students to begin keeping a list of events, experiences, or activities that could be used for an essay topic.

RESOURCES

- grammar.yourdictionary.com/style-and-usage/active-voice-adds-impact-to-your-writing.html: Active Voice Adds Impact to Your Writing
- https://www.collegeessayadvisors.com/youtube-tutorials/: College Essay Tutorials
- https://youtu.be/i6Frezoz458: Cliché Essay Topics

Slide #1

College Essays
Part 2

Slide #2

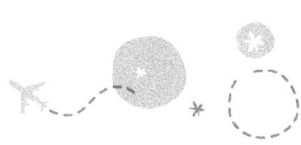

Common App Prompts

1. Some students have a background, identity, interest, or talent that is so meaningful they believe their application would be incomplete without it. If this sounds like you, then please share your story.
2. The lessons we take from obstacles we encounter can be fundamental to later success. Recount a time when you faced a challenge, setback, or failure. How did it affect you, and what did you learn from the experience?
3. Reflect on a time when you questioned or challenged a belief or idea. What prompted your thinking? What was the outcome?
4. Describe a problem you've solved or a problem you'd like to solve. It can be an intellectual challenge, a research query, an ethical dilemma—anything that is of personal importance, no matter the scale. Explain its significance to you and what steps you took or could take to identify a solution.
5. Discuss an accomplishment, event, or realization that sparked a period of personal growth and a new understanding of yourself or others.
6. Describe a topic, idea, or concept you find so engaging that it makes you lose all track of time. Why does it captivate you? What or who do you turn to when you want to learn more?
7. Share an essay on any topic of your choice. It can be one you've already written, one that responds to a different prompt, or one of your own design.

Slide #3

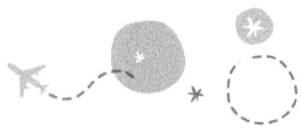

Sample Essay #1

I have always wanted to save the world. As I child I would dream of swooping in at the eleventh hour to save my city from certain destruction. Resplendent in my sparkly pink cape, I would watch with pride as the citizens cheered while the villain was led away in handcuffs.

But as I have gotten older saving the world has become a bit more complicated. I have learned that sadly I can't actually fly, and that not everything can be fixed by one person.

When we look at the world from above, with all of its problems and imperfections, the sheer magnitude of what needs to be fixed can be overwhelming. We start believing that because we aren't policy makers, or billionaires, or PhD holders that we can't make a difference. But, something I have learned over the past few years is that when we look a little closer at our own cities, communities and neighborhoods, the problems become much more solvable.

A few years ago, I learned of a problem in my community with personal significance. As a lifelong competitive swimmer, the water has always been my escape. But for others, the water can be deadly. Factors such as poor economic stability and ethnicity can be directly tied to high drowning rates in communities within my city. When I saw the statistics, I was shocked that no one had attempted to solve this problem before. Unlike some of the other issues I saw on the news, these deaths were not caused by a natural disaster or a political uprising, but rather by a lack of education. This problem has a solution: swim lessons.

And so I have traded in my sparkly cape for a swimsuit, and the villain is no longer a person to vanquish, but a knowledge gap to fill. I spent the first semester of my junior year developing a water safety program that partners with a Title I school in my community and offers free swim lessons and water safety instruction to elementary school-aged children. The second semester of my junior year I implemented the program at an elementary school in inner city Atlanta. These kids may live just a few miles from me, but our lives are vastly different. I have realized how important it is for us to get outside of the bubbles that we live in, and to attempt to walk a mile in someone else's shoes.

Throughout this process I have learned that change does not happen overnight, and that the world will not be saved by one person. I may not be able to save the world singlehandedly, but I can save some of the kids in my city. I have learned that no matter how insignificant we think we may be, we all have something to bring to the table, and the world will be better because of it. Change will not come from one person, or even one community, but from all of us using the unique gifts we have been given to better the world around us.

Slide #4

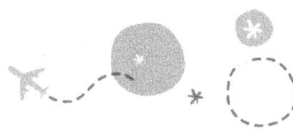

Revised Sample Essay #1

He comes through the door dancing. There is no music playing so he is quite literally dancing to the beat of his own drum. The dancing is not unusual, as he is always moving. Skipping, running, twirling—the only thing he never does is walk. He shimmies his way across the pool deck, and as soon as he sees me his eyes light up.

"Coach SJ!" he yells, narrowly avoiding a passing pedestrian as he twirls over to the edge of the pool. "I want to swim!" he says, bouncing up and down on his toes. I smile and hand him his swimsuit, reminding him not to run on his way to change. His name is Charles, and he is five. Later, after practice is over, he ties a towel around his shoulders like a cape and declares himself a superhero. I watch him pretend to fly and remember how I once longed for superpowers.

I have always wanted to save the world. As a child it seemed simple. All I had to do was put on my sparkly pink cape and the villains would cower before me. But as I have gotten older, reality has complicated my dream. I now know that sadly I can't actually fly and that the world will not be saved by one person. But, as I have learned, this doesn't mean that my voice doesn't matter.

A few years ago I learned of a problem in my community. As a lifelong competitive swimmer, the water has always been my escape, but for others it can be deadly. Factors such as economic stability and cultural conventions are directly tied to high drowning rates in communities within my city. Unlike some of the other issues I saw on the news, these deaths were not caused by a natural disaster or a political uprising, but rather by a lack of education. I saw a solution to this problem: swim lessons.

So I have traded my sparkly cape for a swimsuit, and the villain is no longer a person to vanquish, but rather a knowledge gap to fill. I developed a water safety program that partners with a Title I school to offer free swim lessons and water safety instruction to elementary school-aged children. Hence, SwimUp Atlanta was born.

I implemented the program at an elementary school in inner city Atlanta. This is where I met Charles, the sparkly-eyed kindergartener who twirled his way into my heart. Charles was ecstatic to learn that his constant need to move could be satisfied in the water. It became a place of freedom for him, and it was incredible to see him flourish.

The first step in developing the program was working with a mentor to develop a business plan. During this process I learned how to balance vision and reality while turning an idea into an executable plan of action. After laying the foundation, the next step was advocacy. I honed my communication skills by calling and emailing more strangers than I can count and by giving multiple in-person presentations advocating for the project. Spending the past year consistently advocating for something I believe in has given me a new perspective: even one voice has power. After advocacy came implementation, where I learned how to lead. Leadership, for me, meant learning how to take criticism and to listen to good instruction while still remaining confident in my vision.

Most importantly, I have learned that no matter how insignificant we think we may be, we all have something to bring to the table, and the world will be better because of it. I may not be able to save the world singlehandedly, but I did save Charles. Change will not come from one person, or even one community, but from all of us using the unique gifts we have been given to better the world around us.

Slide #5

Sample Essay #2

Managing to break free from my mother's grasp, I charged. With arms flailing and chubby legs fluttering beneath me, I was the ferocious two year old rampaging through Costco on a Saturday morning. My mother's eyes widened in horror as I jettisoned my churro; the cinnamon sugar rocket gracefully sliced its way through the air while I continued my spree. I sprinted through the aisles, looking up in awe at the massive bulk products that towered over me. Overcome with wonder, I wanted to touch and taste, to stick my head into industrialized freezers, to explore every crevice. I was a conquistador, but rather than searching the land for El Dorado, I scoured aisles for free samples. Before inevitably being whisked away into a shopping cart, I scaled a mountain of plush toys and surveyed the expanse that lay before me: the kingdom of Costco.

Notorious for its oversized portions and dollar fifty hot dog combo, Costco is the apex of consumerism. From the days spent being toted around in a shopping cart to when I was finally tall enough to reach lofty sample trays, Costco has endured a steady presence throughout my life. As a veteran Costco shopper, I navigate the aisles of foodstuffs, thrusting the majority of my weight upon a generously filled shopping cart whose enormity juxtaposes my small frame. Over time, I've developed a habit of observing fellow patrons tote their carts piled with frozen burritos, cheese puffs, tubs of ice cream, and weight loss supplements. Perusing the aisles gave me time to ponder. Who needs three pounds of sour cream? Was cultured yogurt any more well-mannered than its uncultured counterpart? Costco gave birth to my unfettered curiosity.

While enjoying an obligatory hot dog, I did not find myself thinking about the 'all beef' goodness that Costco boasted. I instead considered finitudes and infinitudes, unimagined uses for tubs of sour cream, the projectile motion of said tub when launched from an eighty-foot shelf or maybe when pushed from a speedy cart by a scrawny seventeen-year-old. I contemplated the philosophical: If there exists a thirty-three ounce jar of Nutella, do we really have free will? I experienced a harsh physics lesson while observing a shopper who had no evident familiarity of inertia's workings. With a cart filled to overflowing, she made her way towards the sloped exit, continuing to push and push while steadily losing control until the cart escaped her and went crashing into a concrete column, 52" plasma screen TV and all. Purchasing the yuletide hickory smoked ham inevitably led to a conversation between my father and me about Andrew Jackson's controversiality. There was no questioning Old Hickory's dedication; he was steadfast in his beliefs and pursuits – qualities I am compelled to admire, yet his morals were crooked. We both found the ham to be more likeable-and tender.

I adopted my exploratory skills, fine tuned by Costco, towards my intellectual endeavors. Just as I sampled buffalo chicken dip or chocolate truffles, I probed the realms of history, dance and biology, all in pursuit of the ideal cart–one overflowing with theoretical situations and notions both silly and serious. I sampled calculus, cross country running, scientific research, all of which are now household favorites. With cart in hand, I do what scares me; I absorb the warehouse that is the world. Whether it be through attempting aerial yoga, learning how to chart blackbody radiation using astronomical software, or dancing in front of hundreds of people, I am compelled to try any activity that interests me in the slightest.

My intense desire to know, to explore beyond the bounds of rational thought; this is what defines me. Costco fuels my insatiability and cultivates curiosity within me at a cellular level. Encoded to immerse myself in the unknown, I find it difficult to complacently accept the "what"; I want to hunt for the "whys" and dissect the "how's". In essence, I subsist on discovery.

Slide #6

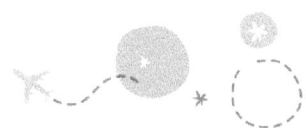

Sample Essay #2—Strong Verbs

Managing to break free from my mother's grasp, I charged. With arms flailing and chubby legs fluttering beneath me, I was the ferocious two year old rampaging through Costco on a Saturday morning. My mother's eyes widened in horror as I jettisoned my churro; the cinnamon sugar rocket gracefully sliced its way through the air while I continued my spree. I sprinted through the aisles, looking up in awe at the massive bulk products that towered over me. Overcome with wonder, I wanted to touch and taste, to stick my head into industrialized freezers, to explore every crevice. I was a conquistador, but rather than searching the land for El Dorado, I scoured aisles for free samples. Before inevitably being whisked away into a shopping cart, I scaled a mountain of plush toys and surveyed the expanse that lay before me: the kingdom of Costco.

Notorious for its oversized portions and dollar fifty hot dog combo, Costco is the apex of consumerism. From the days spent being toted around in a shopping cart to when I was finally tall enough to reach lofty sample trays, Costco has endured a steady presence throughout my life. As a veteran Costco shopper, I navigate the aisles of foodstuffs, thrusting the majority of my weight upon a generously filled shopping cart whose enormity juxtaposes my small frame. Over time, I've developed a habit of observing fellow patrons tote their carts piled with frozen burritos, cheese puffs, tubs of ice cream, and weight loss supplements. Perusing the aisles gave me time to ponder. Who needs three pounds of sour cream? Was cultured yogurt any more well-mannered than its uncultured counterpart? Costco gave birth to my unfettered curiosity.

While enjoying an obligatory hot dog, I did not find myself thinking about the 'all beef' goodness that Costco boasted. I instead considered finitudes and infinitudes, unimagined uses for tubs of sour cream, the projectile motion of said tub when launched from an eighty-foot shelf or maybe when pushed from a speedy cart by a scrawny seventeen-year-old. I contemplated the philosophical: If there exists a thirty-three ounce jar of Nutella, do we really have free will? I experienced a harsh physics lesson while observing a shopper who had no evident familiarity of inertia's workings. With a cart filled to overflowing, she made her way towards the sloped exit, continuing to push and push while steadily losing control until the cart escaped her and went crashing into a concrete column, 52" plasma screen TV and all. Purchasing the yuletide hickory smoked ham inevitably led to a conversation between my father and me about Andrew Jackson's controversiality. There was no questioning Old Hickory's dedication; he was steadfast in his beliefs and pursuits – qualities I am compelled to admire, yet his morals were crooked. We both found the ham to be more likeable-and tender.

I adopted my exploratory skills, fine tuned by Costco, towards my intellectual endeavors. Just as I sampled buffalo chicken dip or chocolate truffles, I probed the realms of history, dance and biology, all in pursuit of the ideal cart–one overflowing with theoretical situations and notions both silly and serious. I sampled calculus, cross country running, scientific research, all of which are now household favorites. With cart in hand, I do what scares me; I absorb the warehouse that is the world. Whether it be through attempting aerial yoga, learning how to chart blackbody radiation using astronomical software, or dancing in front of hundreds of people, I am compelled to try any activity that interests me in the slightest.

My intense desire to know, to explore beyond the bounds of rational thought; this is what defines me. Costco fuels my insatiability and cultivates curiosity within me at a cellular level. Encoded to immerse myself in the unknown, I find it difficult to complacently accept the "what"; I want to hunt for the "whys" and dissect the "how's". In essence, I subsist on discovery.

Slide #7

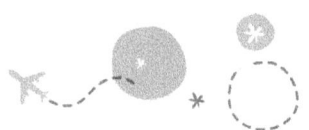

Types of Essays—Narrative and Collage

Narrative—These essays tell a story and are often anecdotal, experiential, and personal—allowing students to express themselves in creative and, quite often, moving ways.

Collage—These essays use multiple parts or separate fragments to tell the whole story.

Slide #8

Best Practice Dos and Don'ts

Do
- Craft an engaging hook
- Use active voice
- Show
- Use descriptive verbs
- Be specific
- Avoid overuse of "I" and "to be" verbs
- Use varied sentence length and structure
- Avoid repetition
- Use your authentic voice

Don't
- Write an autobiography
- Use passive voice
- Tell
- Force humor
- Repeat your resume
- Use overused topics
- Use clichés

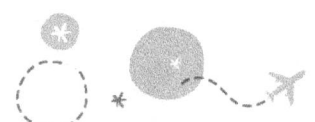

Slide #9

Topics to Avoid

- The Trip
- My Favorite Things
- Miss America
- Pet Death
- Your "Jock" Story
- The 3 Ds—Discipline, Determination, and Diversity

Slide #10

5 College Essays That Suck

Slide #11

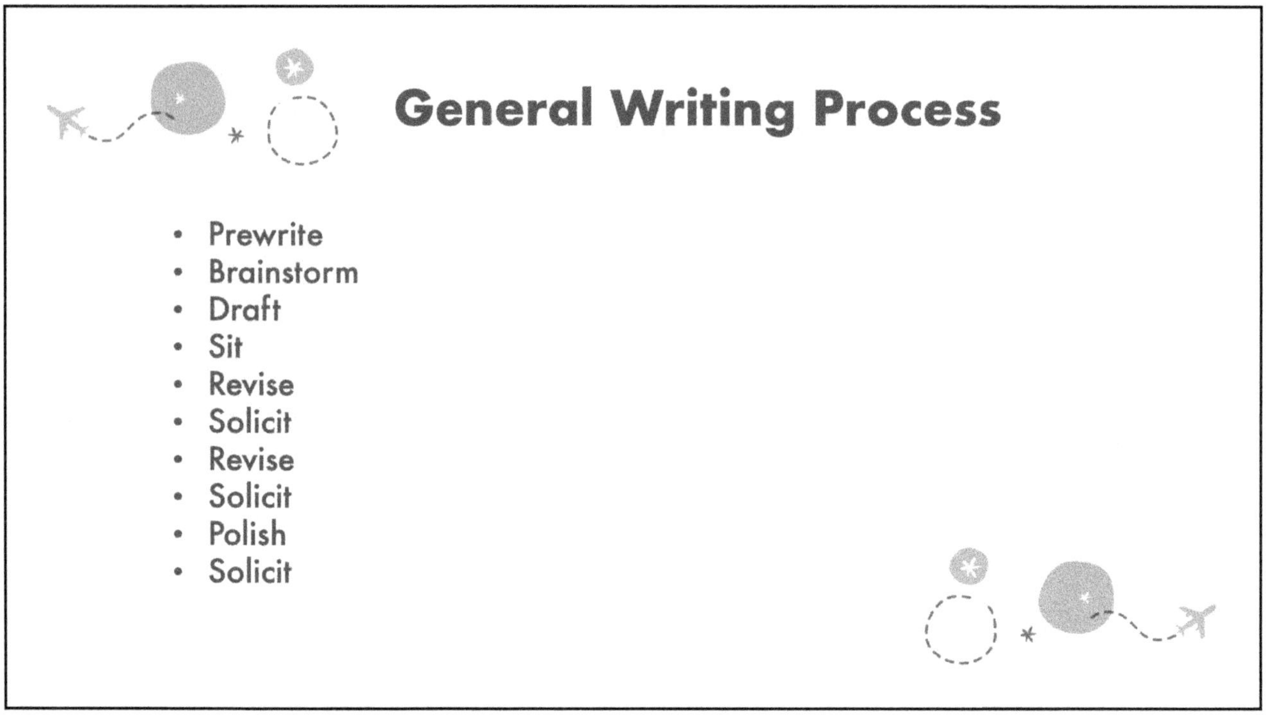

General Writing Process

- Prewrite
- Brainstorm
- Draft
- Sit
- Revise
- Solicit
- Revise
- Solicit
- Polish
- Solicit

Slide #12

- Good writing takes time, so start early
- Think of the Common App essay as a way for admissions committees to get to know me

TAKEAWAYS!

Workshop Five

FAFSA, Part 1

YOUR PASSPORT TO COLLEGE

FAFSA, Part 1

OBJECTIVE:
Students will learn the what, why, when, and how of completing the FAFSA and the basics of financial aid.

SUMMARY:
Students will learn the importance of and how to complete the FAFSA and the basics of financial aid.

MATERIALS:
AV equipment for PowerPoint presentation (download the file from www.tlpnyc.com/your-passport-to-college), stable internet connection, one student handout (*FAFSA, Parts 1 and 2*)

Lesson Vocabulary

FAFSA n. a form completed by current and prospective college students in the United States to determine their eligibility for federal financial aid

financial aid office n. on-campus office that provides assistance to students by providing information on ways to pay for college and administers the award of grants, scholarships, and loans

full-need n. an admission policy by which institutions pledge to meet 100 percent of their students' financial need

scholarship n. free money, which is sometimes based on academic merit, talent, or a particular area of study, that a student does not have to repay

FACILITATOR NOTE:
Familiarize yourself with the ten slides in this lesson, including the embedded videos, and the **Myths . . . About the FAFSA** document in the resources prior to facilitation. Make copies of handouts for students.

WARM-UP: COST OF COLLEGE

- Reiterate to participants that college is their destination. Revisit the passport analogy.
- Ask students to guess how much it costs to earn a four-year college degree? Wait for their responses.
- Inform students that the average cost of earning a four-year degree ranges from $87,000 (public in-state) to $199,500 (private nonprofit). Source: educationdata.org.
- College is expensive, but students should not be deterred by the sticker price.
- There are many ways for students to earn scholarships or to obtain funds through other means to pay for college. There are full-need schools that pledge to meet, without loans, 100 percent of a student's financial need. Admission to these schools is selective, so stress the importance of a stellar academic record.

MAIN ACTIVITY

Part 1: What? (includes a 2:32-minute video)

- Begin PowerPoint presentation. Stay on **slide #1**.
- Ask students if they've heard of the FAFSA. Wait for their responses.
- Tell students that this is the first of two workshops during which they are going to learn about the FAFSA and financial aid.
- Proceed to **slide #2: What Is the FAFSA?** and read aloud the content.
- Proceed to **slide #3: FAFSA Overview**. Tell the students that they will watch a short video that gives a brief overview of the FAFSA. Begin the embedded video (2:32).
- Advise students that you will provide more detail a little later about information covered in the video.
- Tell students that the FAFSA is the gateway to the following types of aid:
  - Grants: Grants, unlike loans, are sources of free money that generally do not have to be paid back. A variety of federal grants is available. The most common is the PELL grant.
  - Work-Study: The Federal Work-Study Program allows students to earn money for school by working part-time on campus. Students earn a paycheck.
  - Loans: Borrowed money that must be repaid with the interest that accrues.
  - Aid for military families: There are special aid programs for being the child of a veteran.

Part 2: Why?

- Present **slide #4: Why Complete the FAFSA.**
- Tell students if they want to find out whether they are eligible to get money for college that they must complete the FAFSA.
- Inform students that the FAFSA is used to determine whether a student is eligible for need-based federal financial aid. If a student is eligible, it is a way to help pay for college.
- Review five reasons to complete the FAFSA:
  1. It's FREE: Be aware—tell students that there are several websites that offer help completing the FAFSA for a fee. <u>Never</u> pay. Free help is available at www.fafsa.gov.
  2. It's easier than ever: Advise students that the IRS Data Retrieval Tool (DRT) allows students and parents to access the required information from their IRS tax returns to complete the FAFSA. The data can be directly transferred into the FAFSA from the IRS website (using the DRT) with just a few clicks.
  3. It takes less than thirty minutes to complete: Let students know that on average it takes twenty-one minutes to complete. It is time well spent because students may qualify for thousands of dollars in financial aid.

4. More people qualify than you think: Encourage students by telling them everyone should fill out the FAFSA. Don't leave any money on the table.
5. You may need it to apply for state and college financial aid and even private scholarships: Tell students that many states, schools, and private scholarships require them to submit the FAFSA before they will consider them for any financial aid they offer; the NY State Tuition Assistance Program (TAP) application is linked from the FAFSA and uses the same year's income information.

Part 3: When?

- Present **slide #5: When to Complete the FAFSA.**
- Tell students that time is of the essence. They should know that available funds are distributed on a first-come, first-served basis.
- Stress to students that October 1 is the first date the FAFSA can be completed. Students should strive to complete the FAFSA as close to October 1 as possible.
- Tell students that each college has its own deadline by which the FAFSA must be completed. Nevertheless, completing the FAFSA earlier is better than later.
- Remind students to make note of these individual college FAFSA deadlines, which are generally well after admission application deadlines.
- Review the reasons to complete the FAFSA as soon as possible after October 1. Ask students to follow along as you read aloud.

Part 4: How? (includes a 3:02-minute video)

- Present **slide #6: How to Complete the FAFSA.**
- Revisit the equipment analogy with students. Just like they need equipment (transcript, test scores, essay, and letters of recommendation) for college applications, tell students that they will need "equipment" to complete the FAFSA.
- Before students watch a video on how to complete the FAFSA, let them know that you will present them with a list of "equipment" they need to complete the FAFSA. Tell students that they will need the following:
    ○ Federal Student Aid Account (also known as FSA ID): It's free at https://studentaid.gov/fsa-id/create-account/launch. It is needed <u>before</u> a student can complete the FAFSA. Students should apply for one at least two days before completing the FAFSA to allow enough time for it to be received.
    ○ SSN for both student and parent(s)
    ○ Driver's license number, if a student has one
    ○ Tax records for student and parents, if the student is a dependent (note: students will need tax records from <u>two</u> years before the academic year for which a student requests aid; for example, 2019 tax records are needed for the 2021–2022 academic year)

- Records of untaxed income, if applicable: If students ask, provide them with the following examples: child support, interest income, veterans' noneducation benefits
- Records of student's assets (money): Saving and checking account balances and values of investments (stocks, bonds, and real estate, excluding a primary residence) on the date the student signs the FAFSA
- List of schools student is interested in attending: Listed schools will automatically receive the FAFSA results electronically
- Present **slide #7: How to Complete the FAFSA** and play the embedded video (3:02).
- Answer any questions students have after the video.

Part 5: What Next? (includes a 3:01-minute video)

- Present **slide #8: What Happens Next?** and play the embedded video (3:01).
- Present **slide #9: Follow-up** and tell students that they will learn what they need to do after they submit their FAFSAs.
- SAR—Student Aid Report: Students will receive an SAR. This is a document that provides basic information about a student's eligibility for federal aid and lists answers to questions on the FAFSA. After completing the FAFSA, students will receive an email link with instructions on how to view their SARs. Students should look to receive this email. Students should note their EFCs on their SARs.
- EFC—Expected Family Contribution: A number that colleges use to determine how much financial aid a student is eligible for.
  - It is not the amount of money a student will have to pay, nor is it the amount of money of federal aid a student will receive.
  - The lower the EFC, the more federal financial aid a student is eligible to receive.
- Verification: Tell students that they need to be on the lookout to see if they've been selected for Verification. Verification is the process to ensure the accuracy of financial aid information submitted on the FAFSA.
  - Students may be selected for Verification because of possible errors, inconsistencies, or other anomalies. Or some students may be randomly selected for verification after they complete the FAFSA.
  - If a student is selected for Verification, colleges will ask the student to complete Verification worksheets. Specific instructions on what needs to be done will be provided.
- Financial aid office: Let students know they should expect to receive a "financial aid package" from each college's financial aid office. The package usually arrives in the spring semester. This package will include the dollar amount students will receive for each of the following categories: grants and/or scholarships, loans, and work-study.
- Email: Remind students to check email regularly, at least once a day, because it is the primary method colleges use to communicate with them. They do not want to miss important deadlines.
- Present **slide #10: Takeaways!**

DISCUSSION QUESTIONS

1. *Have I talked to my parent(s) or guardian(s) about helping me apply for financial aid?*
2. *Do I have or can I obtain the required documents and information to complete the FAFSA?*

CLOSING

- People that can help me with the financial aid process include _____.

EXTENSION ACTIVITY

- Tell students to notify their guidance counselor(s) that they may need assistance with the financial aid process.

RESOURCES

- https://studentaid.gov: Federal Student Aid—Office of the US Department of Education
- https://studentaid.gov/articles/fafsa-myths/: Fifteen Myths We're Busting About the FAFSA Process
- https://studentaid.gov/sites/default/files/creating-using-fsaid.pdf: Creating and Using the FSA ID (English)
- https://studentaid.gov/sites/default/files/creating-using-fsaid-spanish.pdf: Creating and Using the FSA ID (Spanish)
- https://studentaid.gov/articles/10-fafsa-mistakes-to-avoid/: 10 Common FAFSA Mistakes to Avoid
- https://ifap.ed.gov/sites/default/files/attachments/2019-10/2021SARMockupEnglish_1.pdf: Sample SAR (Student Aid Report)
- Twitter: @FAFSA—official account of Federal Student Aid
- https://studentaid.gov/understand-aid/types/grants/teach: Federal TEACH Grant Program for students who are completing or plan to complete coursework needed to begin a career in teaching

NAME:

WORKSHOPS FIVE AND SIX: FAFSA, PARTS 1 AND 2

The FAFSA is the gateway to the following types of federal aid:

G_____

W_____

L_____

I must have an _____ ID before I am able to complete the FAFSA.
I can get one at https://_____.gov.

The FAFSA is available each year on _____.

Circle whether each statement is true or false.
- T / F: I only need to complete the FAFSA one time.
- T / F: It should never cost anything to complete the FAFSA.
- T / F: The most expensive college always costs the most to attend.

_____ aid comes directly from colleges from resources provided by donors, departments, or public sources.

NOTES

_____
_____
_____
_____
_____
_____
_____
_____
_____

ANSWERS

WORKSHOPS FIVE AND SIX: FAFSA, PARTS 1 AND 2

The FAFSA is the gateway to the following types of federal aid:

G_____ Grants _____

W_____ Work-study _____

L_____ Loans _____

I must have an _____ FSA _____ ID before I am able to complete the FAFSA.

I can get one at https://_____ studentaid _____.gov.

The FAFSA is available each year on _____ October 1 _____.

Circle whether each statement is true or false.
- T /(F): I only need to complete the FAFSA one time.
- (T)/ F: It should never cost anything to complete the FAFSA.
- T /(F): The most expensive college always costs the most to attend.

_____ Institutional _____ aid comes directly from colleges from resources provided by donors, departments, or public sources.

Slide #1

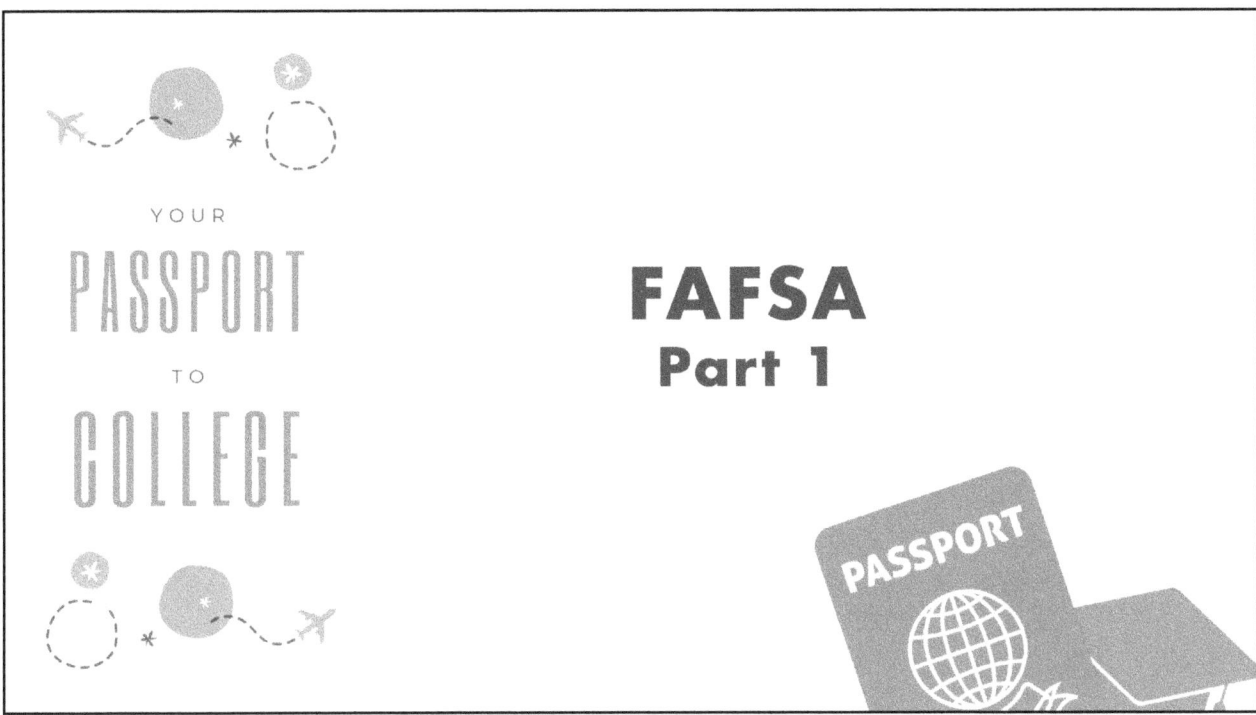

Slide #2

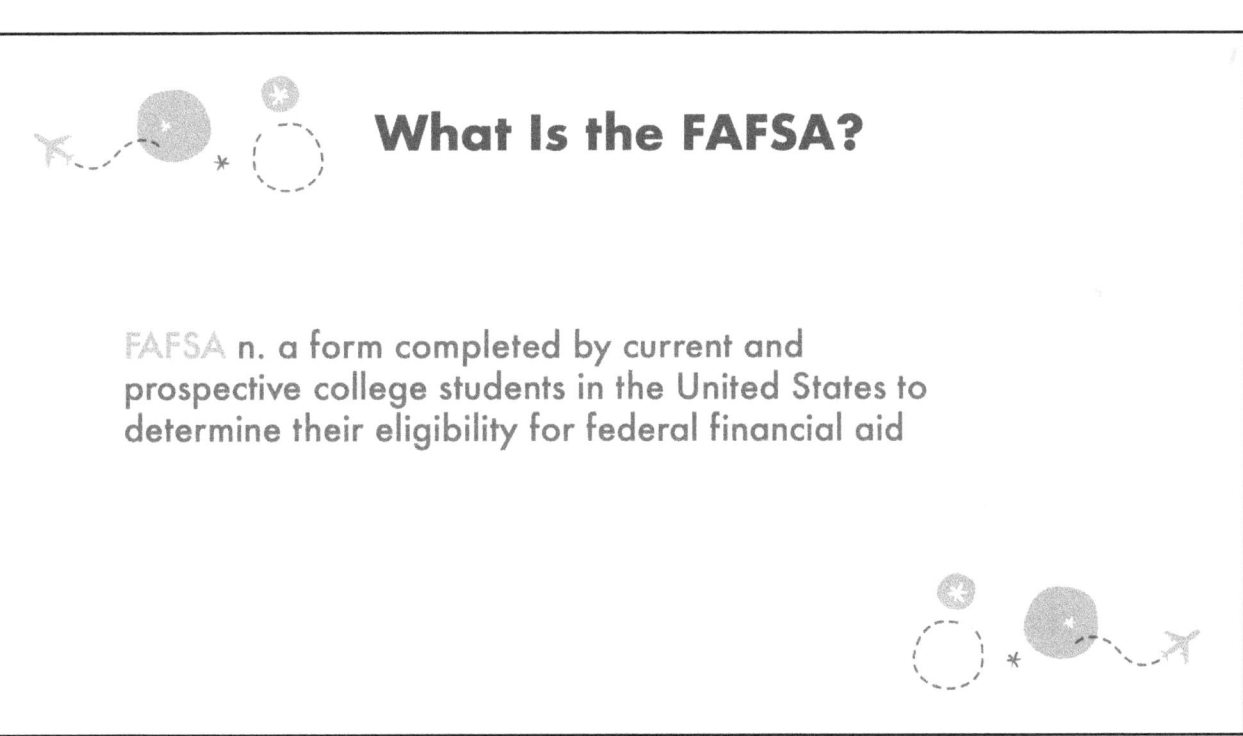

Slide #3

FAFSA Overview

Slide #4

Why Complete the FAFSA?

1. It's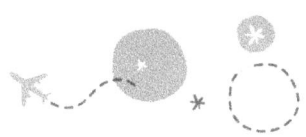
2. It's easier than ever
3. It takes less than thirty minutes
4. More people qualify than you think
5. You may need it to apply for state and college financial aid and private scholarships

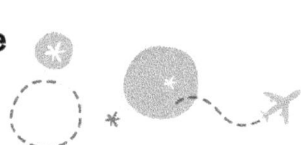

Slide #5

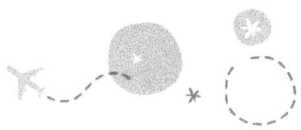
When to Complete the FAFSA
October 1

Reasons to complete the FAFSA as soon as possible after October 1:

1. You'll have a better chance of receiving aid from programs with limited funds, like federal work-study and institutional grants.
2. You can complete the FAFSA before your college applications—just include colleges you plan to apply to and, if needed, update with additional colleges later.
3. It's easy! Most students and families can use the IRS Data Retrieval Tool to complete the income questions.
4. You'll learn about financial aid eligibility early in the admissions process and can make more informed decisions about what colleges apply to.
5. You're sure to meet all of your prospective colleges' priority financial aid filing deadlines.
6. If you apply for early decision or early action, you'll get finalized financial aid award information soon after acceptance notification.
7. If you're planning to apply for any private scholarships that require you to be Pell eligible, you'll know your eligibility right away.
8. You'll be able to explore the financial impact of a college choice well before the May 1 deadline for accepting a spot.
9. If borrowing is needed, federal loans are best, and the only way to apply for those is through the FAFSA.

Slide #6

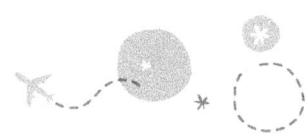
How to Complete the FAFSA

Equipment needed to complete the FAFSA:

1. FSA account—also known as FSA ID
2. Social security number
3. Driver's license number
4. Tax records from two years ago
5. Records of your assets
6. List of colleges you plan on applying to

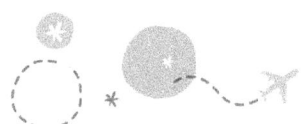

Slide #7

Slide #8

Slide #9

Follow-up

- **SAR**—Student Aid Report
- **EFC**—Estimated Family Contribution
- Verification
- Financial aid office
- Email

Slide #10

TAKEAWAYS!

- Complete the FAFSA on October 1 or as soon thereafter as possible
- Use FREE resources, if necessary, to help complete the FAFSA

Workshop Six

FAFSA, Part 2

YOUR PASSPORT TO COLLEGE

FAFSA, Part 2

OBJECTIVE:
Students will learn the difference between institutional and external scholarships and the role the FAFSA plays in applying for institutional and external funds. Students will also learn how to strategically search for internal scholarship opportunities and full-need institutions as ways to pay for college.

SUMMARY:
Students will learn the importance of the FAFSA in applying for state and private funds and how to search for internal scholarship opportunities.

MATERIALS:
AV equipment for PowerPoint presentation (download the file from www.tlpnyc.com/your-passport-to-college) and stable internet connection

Lesson Vocabulary

CSS Profile n. the College Scholarship Service (CSS) Profile is an online application created by the College Board (the SAT people) that allows college students to apply for nonfederal financial aid

demonstrated need n. the difference between total college costs and the family's ability to pay

external scholarship n. a scholarship funded by a source other than an institution; funding sources may be companies, individuals, or organizations

FAFSA n. a form completed by current and prospective college students in the United States to determine their eligibility for federal student financial aid

financial aid office n. on-campus office that provides assistance to students by providing information on ways to pay for college and administers the award of grants, scholarships, and loans

full-need n. an admission policy by which institutions pledge to meet 100 percent of their students' financial need

internal scholarship n. a scholarship or other funds offered directly through an institution from resources provided by donors, departments, or public sources

need blind adj. an admission policy that does not consider an applicant's financial status when deciding whether to accept them

FACILITATOR NOTE:
Familiarize yourself with the six slides in this lesson, including the embedded video, prior to facilitation. Make copies of handouts for students.

WARM-UP: SCHOLARSHIPS—INTERNAL AND EXTERNAL

- Inform students that this is the second part of the FAFSA workshop. Relate the FAFSA to the passport analogy. The FAFSA can lead to funding for students' trips to their final destinations— their respective colleges.
- Ask students to explain the difference between *internal* versus *external*. Wait for responses.
- Tell students that in the world of financial aid, they may hear the terms *internal* and *external*. Ex: *internal scholarships/aid* and *external scholarships/aid*.
- Review the definitions of *internal scholarship* and *external scholarship* with students.
- Let students know that many internal and external scholarships require that students complete the FAFSA. Remind students that they learned how to complete the FASA during the last workshop.
- Tell students that they may also hear the terms *demonstrated need*, *need blind*, and *full-need*.

MAIN ACTIVITY

Part 1: Institutional Scholarships and Aid

- Begin PowerPoint presentation with **slide #1**.
- Proceed to **slide #2**. Explain to students that colleges and universities have their own pots of money to award students. This is institutional aid because it comes from within the school.
- Inform students that these funds may come from a variety of sources. Ex: *individual* or *corporate donors*, *states*, and *nonprofit organizations*.
- Tell students that they need to actively look for these funds.
- Let students know that they can use Google and individual college websites to search. The right queries will yield fruitful results. Some colleges award more institutional aid than others. The key is to keep looking.
- Proceed to **slide #3**: **How to Find Institutional Scholarships or Aid** and read its content.
- Advise participants that the FAFSA is sometimes required to receive institutional aid. Point out to students that, in addition, an application for financial aid separate from the admission application may be required.
- Mention the CSS Profile—College Scholarship Service Profile—to students. Let them know that some colleges may require it in addition to the FAFSA.
  - The CSS Profile is a form administered by the College Board that approximately four hundred colleges (primarily selective, private institutions) use to determine eligibility for financial assistance.
  - The CSS Profile is more detailed than the FAFSA and it costs $25 (waivers are available for eligible students) to complete.

- ○ Encourage students to speak with their counselors if they apply to schools that require the CSS Profile or if they want to find out whether they are eligible for a waiver.

Part 2: Full Demonstrated Need

- Proceed to **slide #4: Full Demonstrated Need** and read the contents.
- Tell students that the goal of need-based aid is to reduce or eliminate financial barriers to attending college.
- Inform students that some colleges guarantee to meet the full demonstrated financial need of admitted students. These colleges have sufficient resources to make most admission decisions independent of financial aid consideration.
- Tell students that if their families cannot afford college that they should strategically search for schools that meet full demonstrated need.
- Explain to students that full demonstrated need means that a college will award aid to help families cover the difference between what the college calculates families should pay and the actual cost of attendance. The aid will come in a package that may include grants, loans, and work-study jobs.
- Tell students that the key is for them to search for schools that meet need <u>without loans</u>. Paying for college without loans is ideal.
- Inform students that they can find these schools with the help of Google by searching: "schools that meet full financial need without loans." Most of the schools are highly selective.

Part 3: Award Letters (includes two videos, 1:33 and 1:40 minutes)

- Proceed to **slide #5: Award Letters**
- Inform students that provided they complete the FAFSA and any required institutional financial aid applications, they will receive a "package," via email or snail mail, that tells them what money they have been offered. They will receive a package from each school.
- Tell students that the packages will include dollar amounts in the following categories: grants, scholarships, loans, and work-study.
- Let students know that the packages usually arrive early in the spring semester.
- Stress to students that they need to keep all award letters and seek help determining which package is best. It is possible that the most expensive school on a student's list might not cost the most.
- Tell students that you will show two short videos. The first video explains how to read a financial aid award letter. Play video (1:33) embedded on slide. https://www.youtube.com/watch?v=GA7TRkmGIyc
- Inform students that now they will watch the second video (1:40). It is from the NY HESC regarding its Financial Aid Comparison Tool. https://www.youtube.com/watch?v=GrAsYJWzf0o

Part 4: External Scholarships

- Explain to students that they can apply for aid from sources other than the colleges to which they apply. Some sources may include businesses, community groups, foundations, or other entities.
- Remind students that the FAFSA may be required. Each external entity decides whether the FAFSA is required for the distribution of its awards.
- Tell students that external scholarships are beyond the scope of this workshop, but caution them that they should <u>never</u> pay for scholarship search services.
- Encourage students to see their counselors for free scholarship resources. Advise them to be persistent.
- Present **slide #6: Takeaways!**

DISCUSSION QUESTIONS

1. *Have I talked to my parent(s) or guardian(s) about helping me apply for financial aid?*
2. *Do I have or can I obtain the required documents and information to complete the FAFSA?*

CLOSING

- People that can help me with the financial aid process include _____.

EXTENSION ACTIVITY

- Tell students to begin researching internal and external scholarship opportunities.
- Tell students to begin researching colleges and universities that meet full demonstrated need.

RESOURCES

- https://studentaid.gov: Federal Student Aid—Office of the US Department of Education
- https://studentaid.gov/articles/evaluating-financial-aid-offers/: 13 Things to Know When Evaluating Your Financial Aid Offers
- https://studentaid.gov/sites/default/files/dont-get-scammed.pdf: Don't Get Scammed on Your Way to College: Avoid financial aid fraud
- Twitter: @FAFSA—official account of Federal Student Aid

Slide #1

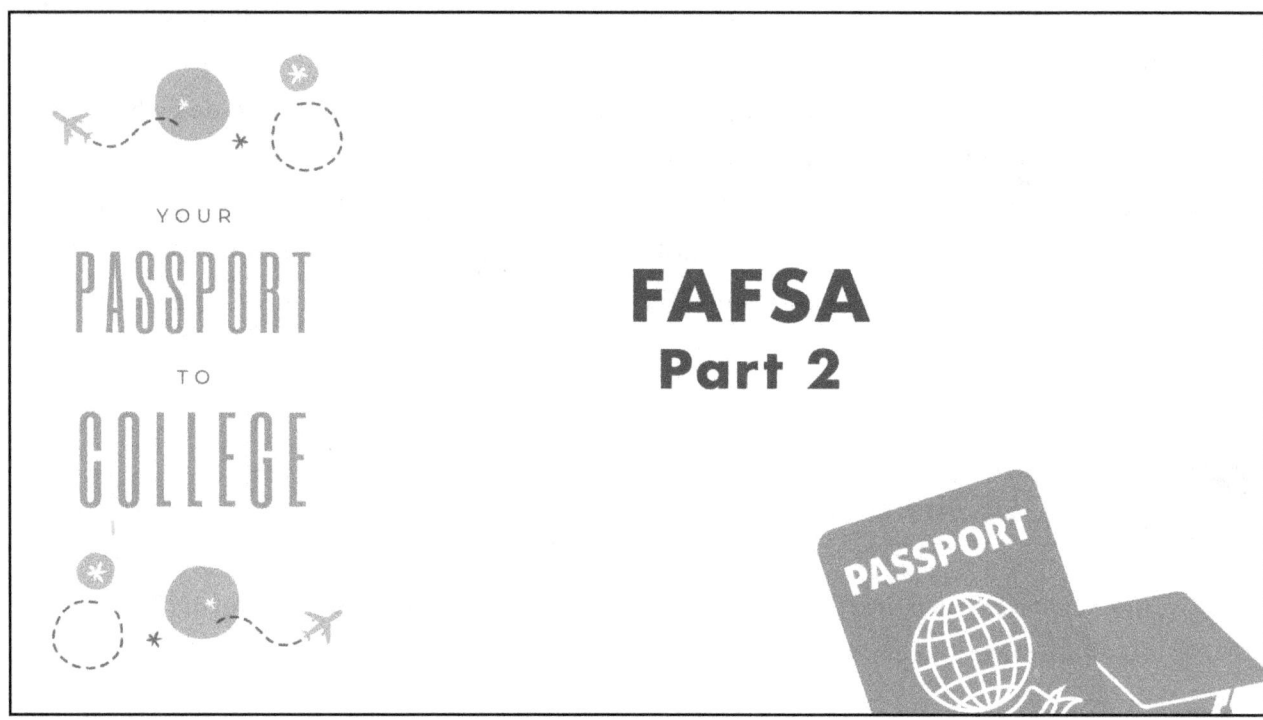

Slide #2

Slide #3

How to Find Institutional Scholarships or Aid

Sample Google queries:
- freshman scholarship [insert name of institution]
- first gen scholarship [insert name of institution]
- diversity scholarship [insert name of institution]
- merit scholarship [insert name of institution]

Queries using the search function on college home pages:
- freshman scholarship
- scholarships
- diversity scholarship

Specific college departments:
- Peruse department home pages to find scholarship opportunities in your chosen major or field

Slide #4

Full Demonstrated Need

Sampling of colleges and universities that meet full demonstrated need, without loans:
- Amherst College (MA)
- Bowdoin College (MA)
- Brown University (RI)
- Columbia University (NY)
- Davidson College (NC)
- Harvard University (MA)
- Massachusetts Institute of Technology (MA)
- Pomona College (CA)
- Princeton University (NJ)
- Stanford University (CA)
- Swarthmore College (PA)

There are more!

Slide #5

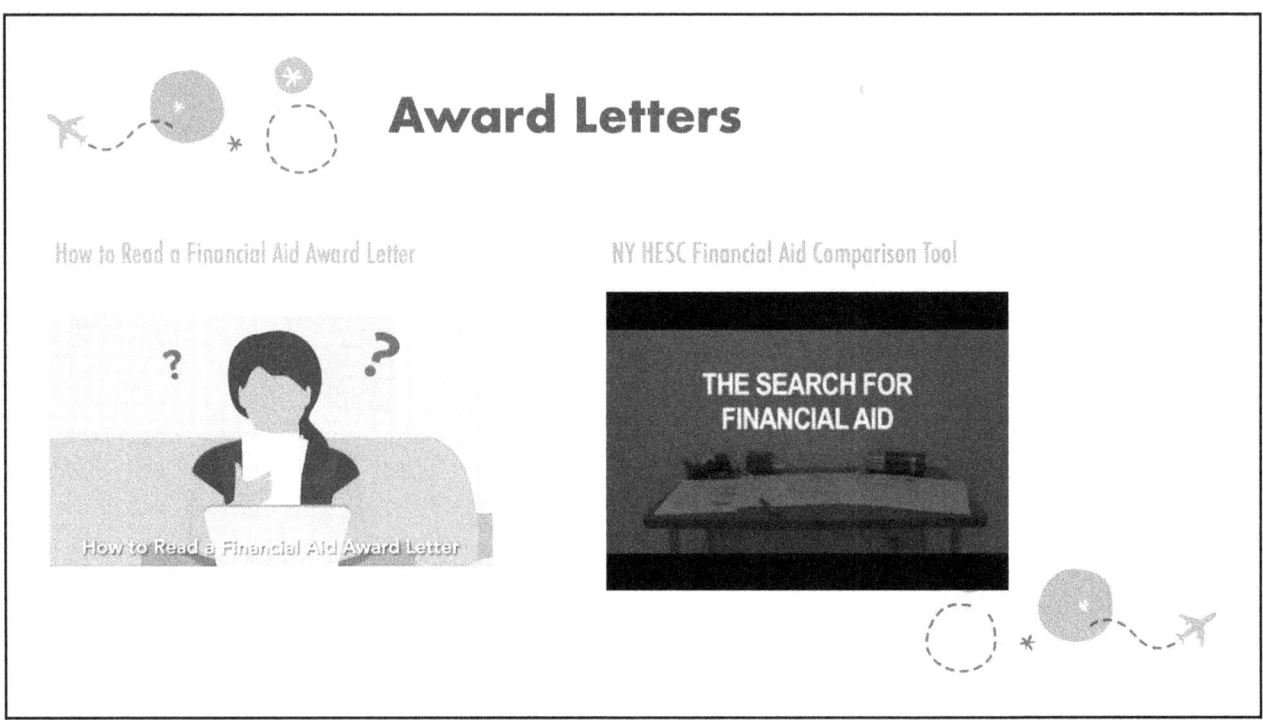

Slide #6

Workshop Seven

Parents

YOUR PASSPORT TO COLLEGE

Parents

OBJECTIVE:
Participants will learn the roles they can play to best assist their students during the college application process and the importance of and how to complete the FAFSA. Participants will also begin to visualize their students as college co-eds.

SUMMARY:
Through a passport analogy, participants will learn how to effectively assist their students during the college application process and how to complete the FAFSA.

MATERIALS:
AV equipment for PowerPoint presentation (download the file from www.tlpnyc.com/your-passport-to-college) and stable internet connection

Lesson Vocabulary

bachelor's degree n. a college degree usually completed in four years of full-time study; most common are bachelor of arts (BA), awarded to students who major in the arts and humanities, and bachelor of science (BS), awarded to students who major in science, technology, or business

FAFSA n. a form completed by current and prospective college students in the United States to determine their eligibility for federal financial aid

first-generation student n. a student both of whose parents did not complete a bachelor's degree, or in the case of students who live with and are supported by only one parent, a student whose only such parent did not complete a bachelor's degree (note: definition may vary by college)

four-year institution n. public or private colleges and universities with undergraduate degree programs that lead to a bachelor's degree in a specific area of study

two-year institution n. a public or private college that provides two-year courses of study that end with students earning an associate's degree; sometimes referred to as a junior or community college and may include a vocational school or technical college

vocational school n. an educational institution whose mission is to equip students with skills needed to enter the workforce by training them for a specific line of work; less academic and more job-focused than a four-year institution

FACILITATOR NOTE:
Familiarize yourself with the ten slides in the PowerPoint, including the embedded videos, prior to facilitation.

WARM-UP: PASSPORT ANALOGY

- Welcome parents and thank them for their time. Let them know that their time is an investment in their students' futures.
- Inform parents that their students have been attending college application workshops based on a passport theme. Advise parents that they can ask their students about their destinations, equipment, itineraries, and timelines.
- Tell parents that students were told passports provide access to see the world and exposure to new places and different people the same way that college provides access to a whole new world and exposure to different places and people. This is true even for those students who choose to attend college locally.
- Advise parents now is the time to see how they fit into the passport analogy.
- Share with parents that they are the travel agents in the passport analogy. Just as the primary responsibility of a travel agent is to make the process of travel planning easier for their clients and to ensure they experience the best trip possible, parents can likewise play a supporting role for their college-bound students.
- Warn parents that some students will require more parental assistance, while others will thrive throughout the college application season with less parental involvement.
- Let parents know that you will walk them through how to best support their students.

MAIN ACTIVITY

Part 1: Support (includes a 2:33-minute video)

- Begin PowerPoint presentation. Stay on **slide #1**.
- Let parents know that the college application process is an exciting, but often stressful, time for students.
- Present **slide #2: Let's Get Your Student Ready for College**. Tell parents that they will watch a short video (2:33) greeting from former First Lady Michelle Obama regarding this phase in their students' lives.
- Point out to parents that Mrs. Obama mentioned the FAFSA more than once. Let them know that you will introduce (and review for some) the FAFSA during this workshop. First you will discuss how parents can best support their students.

- Advise parents that the college application process is a months-long process with many moving parts and that their support during this season is critical.
- Let parents know that students may become overwhelmed with forms to complete, essays to write, letters of recommendation to request, standardized tests to take, and more.
- Tell parents that support will look different for each student and household.
- Inform parents that you will review eleven ways for them to provide support.
- Present **slide #3: 11 Ways to Support Your Student** with the following content:
    1. <u>Advocate</u>: Encourage parents to reach out (in person, via email, or by phone call) to their students' school counselors and let the counselors know that they'd like to partner with them during the college application process. Students should take the lead with regard to working with their counselors; however, parental intervention may be required if a student encounters a nonresponsive, overworked, or inept counselor. This is where parental advocacy comes in. Encourage parents to make their presence known. Hold counselors accountable. Tell parents not to be afraid to let counselors know what they expect with regard to helping their students during the application process. Stay in regular touch with counselors. Be sure to thank them for their service when they are doing a good job.
    2. <u>Encourage</u>: Let parents know this can be a stressful time for students. Parents should provide words of encouragement to their students by reassuring students that they are capable of going to college and that they will get through the application process. Parents should also encourage their students to take ownership of the process. Let students interact with college admissions officers. Admonish parents that they should refrain from contacting admissions officers on behalf of their students. Do not do it. Tell parents this will reflect poorly on their students.
    3. <u>Listen</u>: Tell parents that unsolicited advice is not always welcome. Remind them that teens often just need a listening ear without judgement.
    4. <u>Support</u>: Let parents know there are a couple of tangible ways to provide support. Some students are well-organized and are good at time management, while many are not. Parents know their students best. Encourage parents to serve as "administrative assistants" if necessary. This may entail helping students keep all of their application documents organized. Tell parents the biggest and most important way for parents to support their students is by providing financial support. This does not necessarily mean doling out money. Parents can support their students financially by filing their taxes on time and by providing the necessary financial information for the FAFSA. This financial support cannot be overstated, especially for low-income and/or first-generation households.
    5. <u>Engage</u>: Advise parents it is not their role to take over their students' college application process, but it is helpful for them to know what is going on. This may

include being aware of deadlines just in case students need remindng. It is best for parents to be aware and not in the dark.

6. Focus: Tell parents they can help their students by reminding them to focus on the big picture—going to college. Students sometimes get caught up in attending their dream schools or attached to their first-choice colleges. Parents can reassure their students that there are no perfect schools. Tell parents to reassure their students that there are many schools where they will be perfectly happy.

7. Build boundaries: Tell parents it is common for students to be on college overload during the application process. College. College. College. It may seem like that is all that people talk about. Constant talk about college is very stressful for most students. They often feel pressure to get accepted at particular schools and get overwhelmed by the entire application process. Let parents know they can help reduce stress and anxiety by setting boundaries when it comes to discussing college with their students. Encourage parents to limit college discussions (ex: *status of applications*) to a weekly meeting. Both parents and students can mentally prepare for a prescheduled discussion. The goal is to limit the amount of time spent discussing college admissions.

8. Refrain: Share with parents that they are often tempted to do much of the talking, including rehashing their college application experiences, during this process. Now is not the time for parents to compare their college application experiences with those of their students. Advise parents that they should refrain from such comparisons. Also, parents should refrain from living vicariously through their children and from judging their parenting efforts during this process. Parents may inadvertently add pressure on their students by adding unfair or superficial parental expectations.

9. Be patient: Remind parents that students change their minds. Let parents know that how a student feels about a college at the start of the school year may not necessarily be the way the student feels in the spring, and that is OK. Parents can support their students by giving them space to change and by allowing them freedom to make their own choices.

10. Be realistic: Tell parents that many students feel pressure to get into a particular college (ex: *a "name brand" school, a parent's alma mater, where friends have been accepted*). Parents can support their students by making sure they have diverse lists of colleges to which to apply. Their lists should include reach, target, and safety schools.

11. Ask for help: Let parents know that the importance of asking for help cannot be overstated. Stress to parents that this is by far the most important way that they can help their students. It does not matter whether a parent has a high school diploma (or not) or an advanced college degree. There is no stigma associated with seeking

help during this process. Stress that the process can be overwhelming for parents who have not attended college, as it is unfamiliar territory filled with unfamiliar vocabulary. As for parents who have graduated from college, chances are that the process has changed dramatically since they applied. Encourage parents to begin thinking about whom they can reach out to for help if necessary.

Part 2: FAFSA (includes two videos, 2:50 and 3:02 minutes)

- Proceed to **slide #4: FAFSA**. Tell parents you will talk about the FAFSA for the rest of the workshop. Refresh parents' memories that Mrs. Obama talked about the FAFSA in the video they watched.
- Proceed to **slide #5: What Is the FAFSA?** and read aloud the content.
- Tell parents that completing the FAFSA is the best way to financially support their students.
- Present **slide #6: FAFSA Form and FSA ID Help for Parents**. Tell parents that they will watch a short video that gives a brief overview of the FAFSA. Begin the embedded video (2:50).
- Inform parents that the FAFSA is the gateway to the following types of aid for their students:
  - Grants: Grants, unlike loans, are sources of free money that generally do not have to be paid back. A variety of federal grants are available. The most common is the PELL grant.
  - Work-study: The Federal Work-Study Program allows students to earn money for school by working part-time on campus. Students earn a paycheck.
  - Loans: Borrowed money that must be repaid with the interest that accrues.
  - Aid for military families: There are special aid programs for being the child of a veteran.
- Present **slide #7: Why Complete the FAFSA.**
- Tell parents that students must complete the FAFSA if they want to find out whether they are eligible to get money for college.
- Inform parents that the FAFSA is used to determine a student's eligibility for federal financial aid. If a student is eligible, it is a way to help pay for college.
- Explain the five reasons their students should fill out the FAFSA:
  1. It's FREE: Be aware—there are several websites that offer help completing the FAFSA for a fee. <u>Never</u> pay. Free help is available at www.fafsa.gov.
  2. It's easier than ever: The IRS Data Retrieval Tool (DRT) allows students and parents to access the required information from their IRS tax returns to complete the FAFSA. The data can be directly transferred into the FAFSA from the IRS website (using the DRT) with just a few clicks.
  3. It takes less than thirty minutes to complete: On average it takes twenty-one minutes to complete. It is time well spent because students may qualify for thousands of dollars in financial aid.

4. More people qualify than you think: Everyone should fill out the FAFSA. Don't leave any money on the table.
5. Students may need it to apply for state and college financial aid and even private scholarships: Many states, schools, and private scholarships require students to submit the FAFSA before they will consider them for any financial aid they offer; the NY State Tuition Assistance Program (TAP) application is linked from the FAFSA and uses the same year's income information.

- Present **slide #8: When to Complete the FAFSA.**
- Tell parents that time is of the essence because available funds are distributed on a first-come, first-served basis.
- Stress to parents that October 1 is the first date the FAFSA can be completed. Students should strive to complete the FAFSA as close to October 1 as possible, so it is imperative that parents have their financial information available as close to that date as possible.
- Tell parents now that they know the what, why, and when of the FAFSA, they will learn the how.
- Present **slide #9: How to Complete the FAFSA.**
- Advise parents that their students have watched a video on how to complete the FAFSA. Inform them that they will watch the same video shortly.
- First, let parents know they will need to have the following information available for their students to complete the FAFSA:
    ○ Driver's license number (if applicable)
    ○ Tax records: Students will need their parents' tax records from two years before the academic year for which a student requests aid
    ○ Records of untaxed income, if applicable: If parents ask, provide them with the following examples: child support, interest income, veterans' noneducation benefits
    ○ Records of parents' assets (money): Saving and checking account balances and values of investments (stocks, bonds, and real estate, excluding a primary residence) on the date the student signs the FAFSA
    ○ SSN: A social security number is not required, because parents' citizenship does not affect a student's eligibility for aid; but an SSN is required to obtain an FSA ID. An FSA ID is required to sign the FAFSA electronically. Students will have to print out the signature page of the FAFSA for their parent(s) to sign if they do not have an FSA ID and submit the FAFSA via mail.
- Begin the embedded video (3:02), and answer any questions parents have afterward.
- Conclude by letting parents know that the FAFSA is potentially the gateway to thousands of dollars in aid for their students. Encourage parents to prioritize providing their students with their financial information in a timely fashion.

- Advise parents that if they prefer not to share their financial information with their students, they can complete the FAFSA for their students. Parents will need to be sure to complete the student section as if they are their students.

Part 3: Miscellaneous

- Advise parents that you will briefly cover three more topics.
- Fee waivers: Inform parents that students may have access to waivers for college applications and standardized tests. Encourage parents to follow-up with their students about obtaining these waivers if paying for these fees is a barrier to applying to college.
- CSS Profile: Introduce parents to the College Scholarship Service Profile. Inform them that it is an online application form that a very small percentage of colleges use, in addition to the FAFSA, to determine eligibility for financial aid. It is much more detailed than the FAFSA, and there is a $25 fee. Let parents know that you want them to be familiar with it in case their students apply to colleges where it is required to determine financial aid.
- First-generation students: Let parents know that many colleges and universities offer special programs for first-generation students. They are sometimes referred to as "first-gen." Advise parents to encourage their students to search for these programs when looking at colleges.
- Present **slide #10: Takeaways!**

DISCUSSION QUESTIONS

1. *Do I have my financial documents and taxes in order to be of benefit to my student?*
2. *Have I spoken with my student about the college application process?*
3. *Have I offered my full support to my student?*

CLOSING

- People or organizations that I can turn to for help during my student's application process include _____.

EXTENSION ACTIVITY

- Encourage parents to establish a relationship with their students' counselors.

RESOURCES

- https://youtu.be/Pn4OECMTh5w: Types of Federal Student Aid
- https://studentaid.gov/sites/default/files/creating-using-fsaid.pdf: Creating and Using the FSA ID (English)
- https://studentaid.gov/sites/default/files/creating-using-fsaid-spanish.pdf: Creating and Using the FSA ID (Spanish)
- https://studentaid.gov/apply-for-aid/fafsa/filling-out/parent-info: Find out who counts as your parent when filing the FAFSA form
- https://studentaid.gov/sites/default/files/financial-aid-and-undocumented-students.pdf: Financial Aid and Undocumented Students: Questions and Answers
- https://secure-media.collegeboard.org/CollegePlanning/media/pdf/BigFuture-Financial-Aid-Checklist-Spanish.pdf: Financial Aid Checklist for Students and Parents (Spanish)
- https://studentaid.gov/sites/default/files/dont-get-scammed.pdf: Don't Get Scammed on Your Way to College: Avoid financial aid fraud
- https://bigfuture.collegeboard.org/get-in/applying-101/college-admission-glossary: College Admission Glossary: Learn the Lingo
- https://rb.gy/n1etab: Questions to Ask Your Counselor

Slide #1

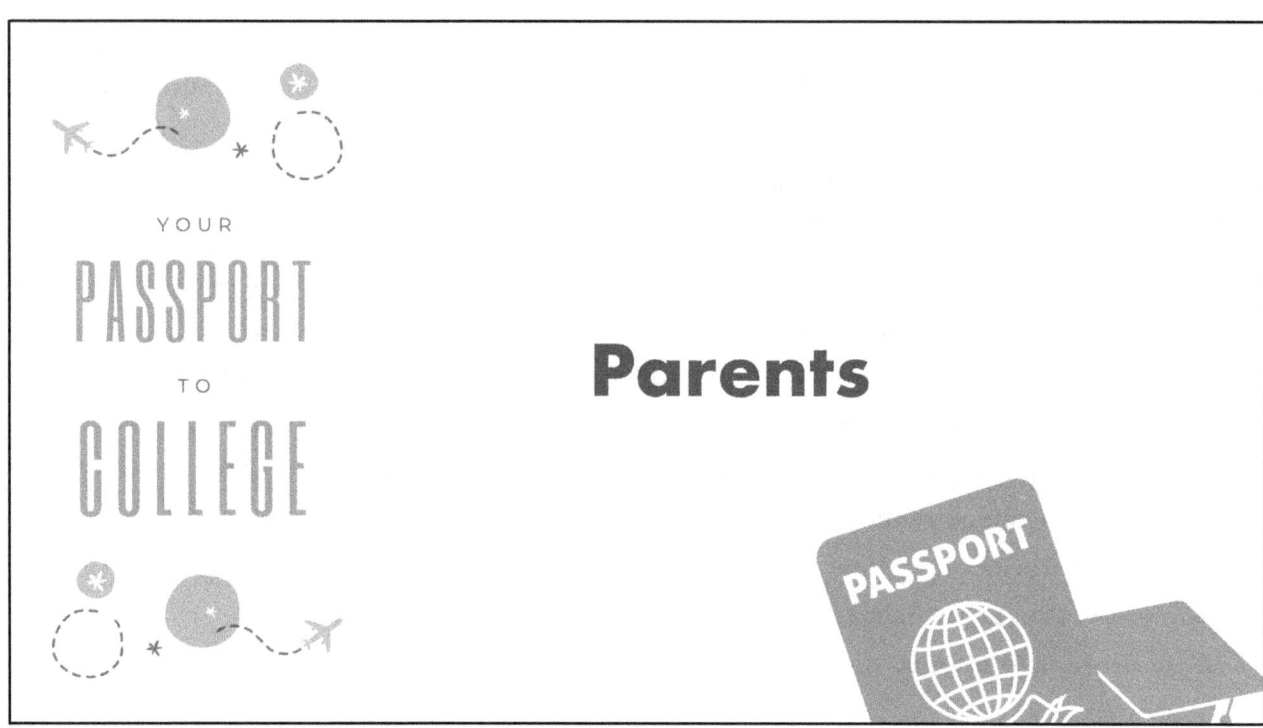

Slide #2

Slide #3

Slide #4

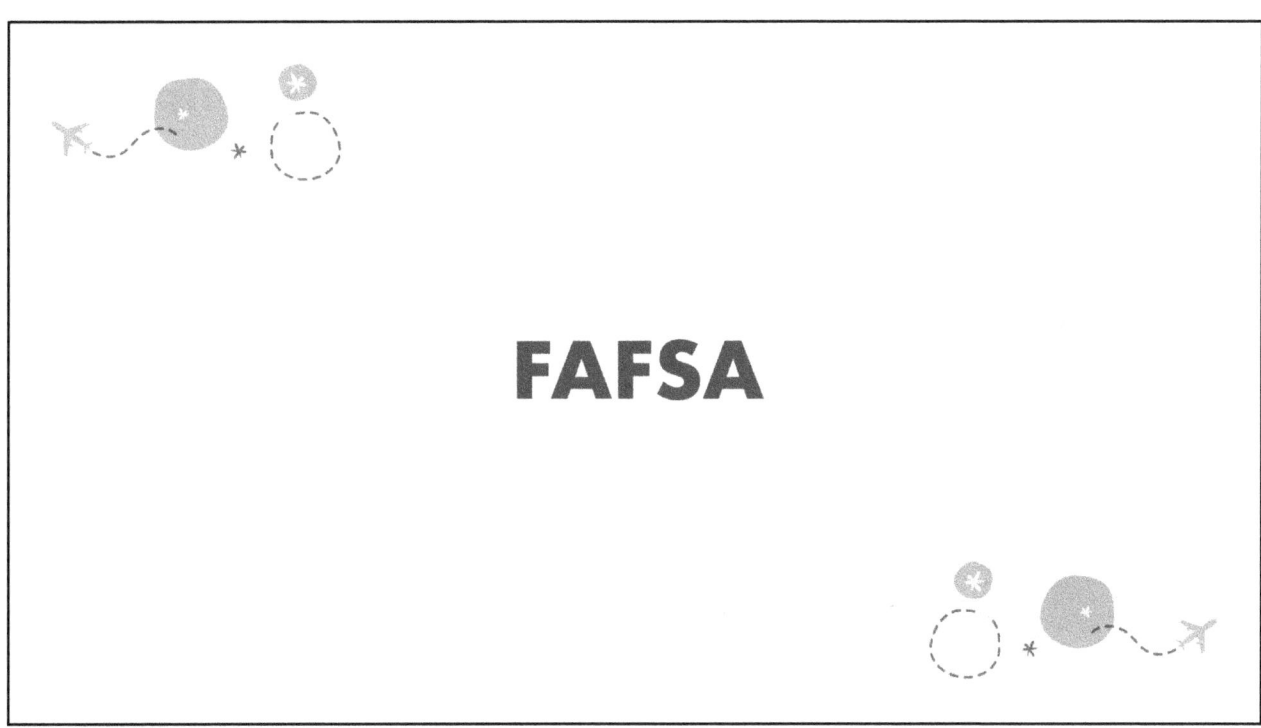

Slide #5

What Is the FAFSA?

FAFSA n. a form completed by current and prospective college students in the United States to determine their eligibility for federal financial aid

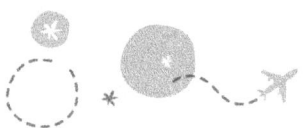

Slide #6

FAFSA Form and FSA ID Help for Parents

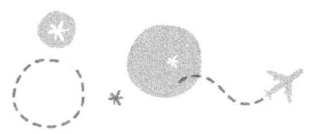

Slide #7

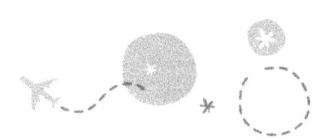
Why Complete the FAFSA
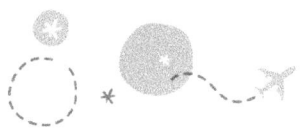

Slide #8

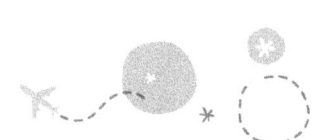
When to Complete the FAFSA
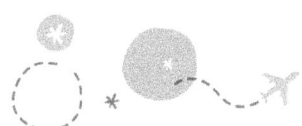

Slide #9

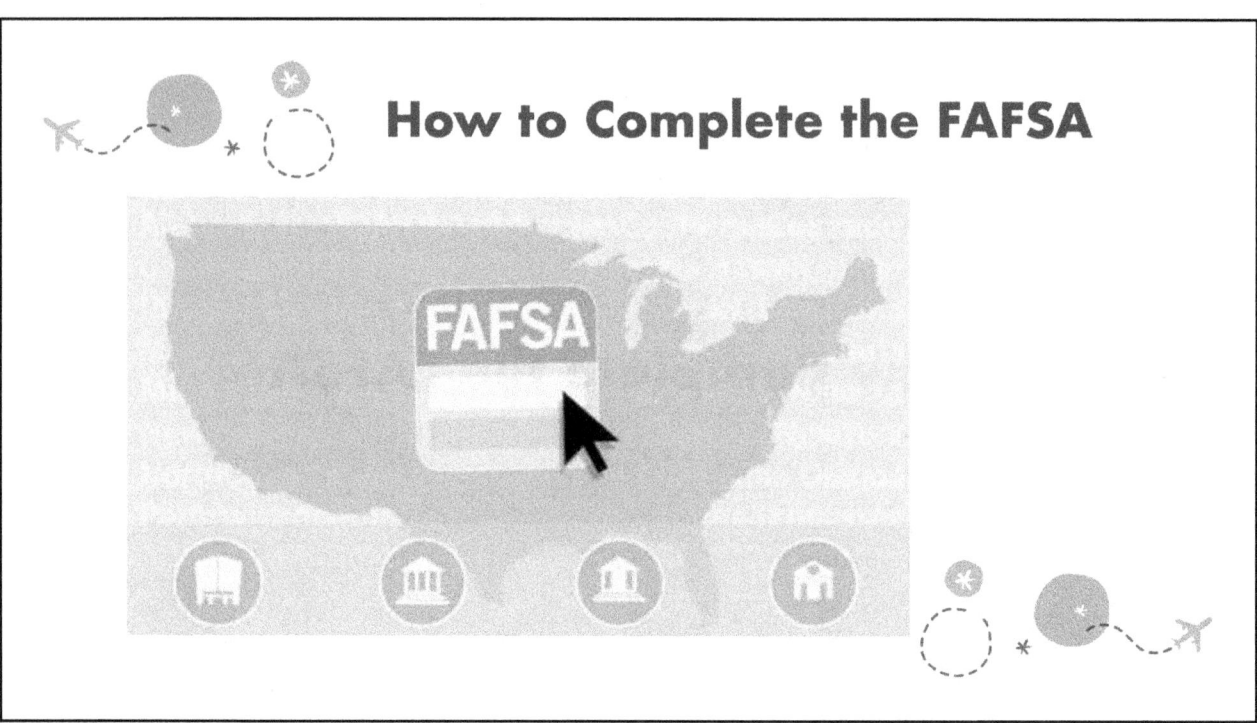

Slide #10

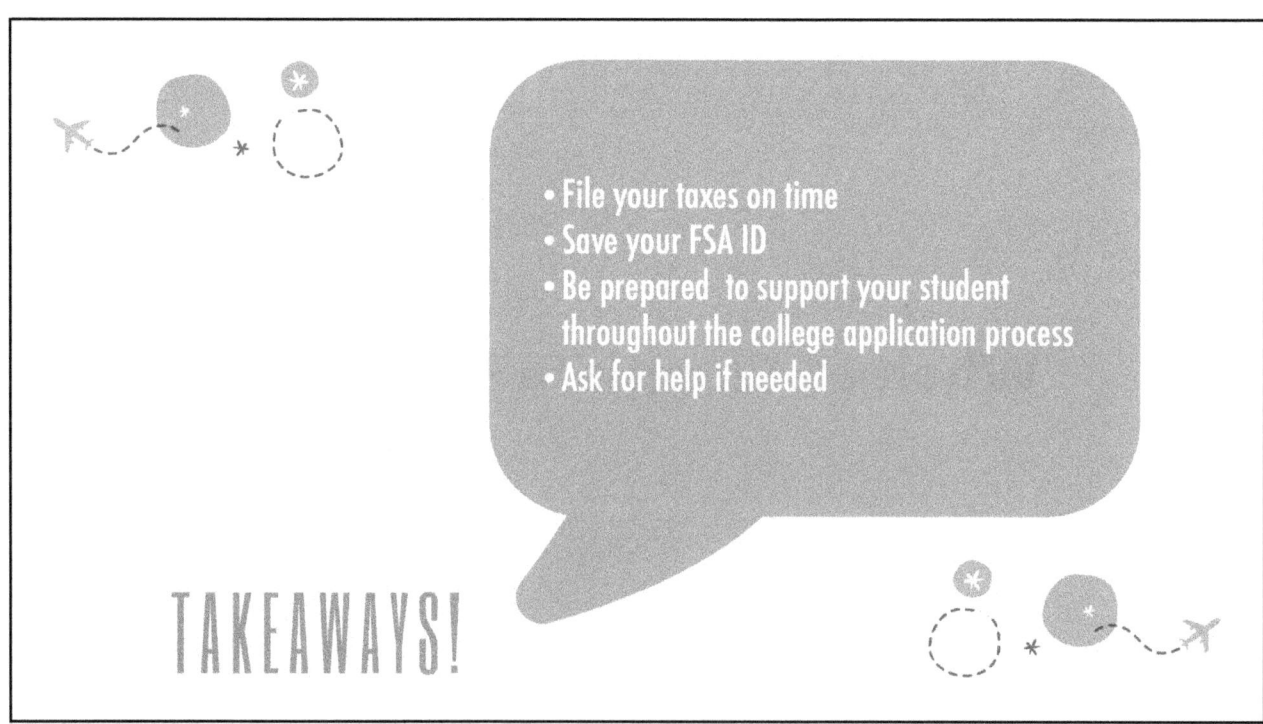

Leadership U. Theoretical Rationale

The Leadership Program's Leadership U. is a comprehensive, equitably designed college and career preparation program for students in grades 4 through 12, intended to complement the academic groundwork being laid by educators.

Early and ongoing preparation is known to be a critical element in increasing the likelihood that students in underserved communities will attend college, and in improving the prospect that all students will thrive in college and beyond (Center for American Progress, 2020). Crucially, intervention is most effective when it starts at an early age—planting the seeds in young minds that college and career choice are realistic options for them—and continues throughout elementary school and high school. Children as young as three years old start to be aware of the jobs and careers of adults around them, and by age nine, they begin to limit the options they see for themselves based on the messages they receive from their community and the media, and the resulting self-concept they develop (Gottfredson, 1981).

The experiences that students have in elementary through high school influence their opportunities to attend college and, in turn, to achieve financial upward mobility as adults. This is particularly true for students of color (US Department of Education, 2016). Educators, increasingly called upon to focus on fostering the development of social and emotional learning (SEL) skills as well as academic achievement, need the support of a well-designed, methodically structured program like Leadership U. to help them narrow the educational achievement gap.

Once students envision themselves in college, it is essential for them to create a plan to achieve their goals by the beginning of high school at the latest (Institute of Education Sciences, 2021; Pathways to College Network, 2007). Crucially, the impact of a college and career plan proves most significant when the plan is reviewed on a regular basis and supported by trusted adults in a student's life. However, typically less than one-quarter of students who make such a plan in ninth grade review their plan yearly, and fewer than half of them have any adult support thereafter (Institute of Education Sciences, 2021). Leadership U. provides both the support of an adult focusing on a future where youth will accomplish their goals and regular yearly reviews of those goals throughout the curriculum.

A variety of factors influence not only whether students will be accepted into a college but also whether they will thrive in college. While academic achievement and content knowledge are necessary elements, they are not sufficient (Pearson, 2022). And while financial viability plays a not insignificant role, essential SEL skills such as resilience, growth mindset, compassion, the ability to set attainable goals, conflict management skills, optimism, and openness to new experiences are often the key to a young person's ability to navigate college life, remain in college, and graduate (Hechinger Report, 2016).

The Leadership U. program provides grade-level-appropriate SEL preparation scaffolded through four curriculum manuals, each tailored to a specific stage of learning and focusing on positive self-ideation, effective communication and collaboration skills, responsible decision-making, and the development of values, attitudes, and healthy relationships that foster postsecondary success (CASEL, 2022). Through integration of the experiential learning cycle, a structured learning sequence that guides multiple styles of learners through experience-based activities (Pfeiffer and Jones, 1975, 1983, as discussed in ERIC, 1993), students gain experience in expressing their views, and have the opportunity to self-reflect and apply lessons learned through participation in the activities.

The Leadership U. syllabus for the final two years of high school incorporates an additional focus on academic and social expectations in college, includes a supplement to guide students through the nuts and bolts of the college application process, and addresses vital skills such as financial literacy and budgeting; understanding how, when, and where to seek support in college; managing academic and social stresses; and developing networking and career goal strategies (Pearson, 2022).

Leadership U.'s approach to preparation for postsecondary life incorporates skills and experiences essential for success in the twenty-first century: investment in education, discovering how you learn best, problem-solving strategies, understanding the benefits of diverse and inclusive communities, optimism, effective techniques for handling challenges, and building self-confidence (Hechinger Report, 2016; Mishkind, 2014). In doing so, this curriculum is uniquely positioned to provide the necessary holistic approach that students need for their future college and career success.

References

CASEL, RAND. *School District Findings: SEL Implementation in Schools* (2022). Retrieved from: https://casel.org/sel-in-schools-nationally-and-in-the-cdi/

Felton, Emmanuel. *The Difference Between Being Eligible for College and Ready for College* (Hechinger Report, 2016). Retrieved from: https://hechingerreport.org/the-difference-between-being-eligible-for-college-and-ready-for-college/

Gibney, Thomas Torre, and Rauner, Mary. *Education and Career Planning in High School: A National Study of School and Student Characteristics and College-Going Behaviors* (US Department of Education, Institute of Education Sciences, National Center for Education Evaluation and Regional Assistance, 2021). Retrieved from: https://ies.ed.gov/ncee/edlabs/regions/west/pdf/REL_2022127.pdf

Gottfredson, Linda. *Using Gottfredson's Theory of Circumscription and Compromise in Career Guidance and Counseling* (2004). Retrieved from: http://www1.udel.edu/educ/gottfredson/reprints/2004theory.pdf

Jimenez, Laura. *Preparing American Students for the Workforce of the Future: Ensuring Every Student's Readiness for College, Career, and Civic Life* (Center for American Progress, 2020). Retrieved from: https://www.americanprogress.org/article/preparing-american-students-workforce-future/

Mishkind, Anne. *Overview: State Definitions of College and Career Readiness* (College & Career Readiness & Success Center at American Institutes for Research, 2014). Retrieved from: https://ccrscenter.org/sites/default/files/CCRS%20Defintions%20Brief_REV_1.pdf

Pathways to College Network, AdLit. *Social Support: An Essential Ingredient to College Success* (2007). Retrieved from: https://www.adlit.org/topics/social-emotional-issues/social-support-essential-ingredient-college-success

Pearson Accelerated Pathways. *5 Reasons College Students Dropout . . . and How We Help!* (2022). Retrieved from: https://www.pearsonaccelerated.com/blog/5-reasons-college-students-dropout-and-how-we-help/

Strong, John R. *Adapting Pfeiffer and Jones' Experiential Learning Model for Classroom Use* (ERIC, Institute of Education Sciences, 1993). Retrieved from: https://eric.ed.gov/?id=ED369115

US Department of Education, Office of Planning, Evaluation and Policy Development. *Advancing Diversity and Inclusion in Higher Education: Key Data Highlights Focusing on Race and Ethnicity and Promising Practices* (2016). Retrieved from: https://www2.ed.gov/rschstat/research/pubs/advancing-diversity-inclusion.pdf

Image Credits

Cover and throughout interior: Margarita Ksenokratova/Shutterstock (globe)

Program Curriculum Support

Curriculum support for all programming is available from The Leadership Program at www.tlpnyc.com/leadership-marketplace.

Empowering Upstanders: A School-Based Bullying Prevention Program

Empowering Upstanders: Student Workbook

Boys 2 MENtors: Curriculum Manual

Boys 2 MENtors: Student Workbook

HERstory: Curriculum Suite

HERstory: Student Writing Companion

Leadership Skills: High School Manual: Violence Prevention Project

Leadership Skills: High School Workbook: Violence Prevention Project

Leadership Skills: Middle School Manual: Violence Prevention Project

Leadership Skills: Middle School Workbook: Violence Prevention Project

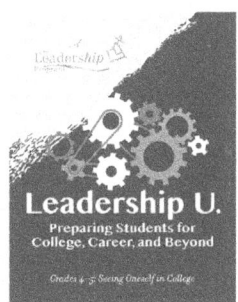
Leadership U. Grades 4–5: Seeing Oneself in College

Leadership U. Grades 6–8: Developing Key Life Skills

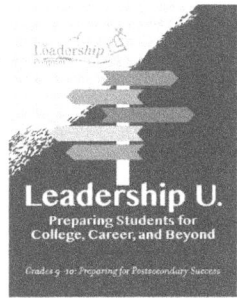
Leadership U. Grades 9–10: Preparing for Postsecondary Success

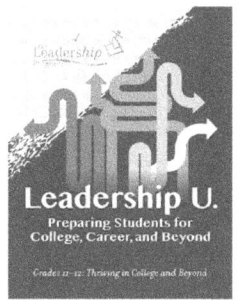
Leadership U. Grades 11–12: Thriving in College and Beyond

Leadership U. High School Supplement: Your Passport to College